Contents

Swordfish

The Fairey Swordfish story is one of an aircraft initially frowned upon when it entered service in 1936, respected by the beginning of the Second World War and deemed legendary by the time peace was declared. The world must have looked on in awe at our powerful Royal Navy and its large carriers and with equal bemusement at the seemingly fragile biplanes, with their single torpedo and light armament upon their decks.

However, the Swordfish was the only torpedo bomber we had in significant numbers at the beginning of the war and it would prove to be so much more. Designed with one role in mind, the Swordfish evolved into one of the most versatile of Naval aircraft. Its slow speed, which was criticised from the outset, proved to be one of its strengths, especially when it came to anti-submarine work, in which it claimed 21 U-boats sunk between April 1940 and December 1944. The later combination of RPs and ASV radar made the Swordfish particularly effective against U-boats and shipping, of which it claimed over 300,000 tons sunk.

Affectionately nicknamed the 'Stringbag', the aircraft achieved an outstanding war record beginning with operations in Norway, where events could have been much different if the Royal Navy was not forced to divert its attention elsewhere. The attack on the Italian harbour at Taranto that crippled the Italian Navy displayed what the aircraft was capable of and that it was clearly not be under estimated. The Swordfish also played an important role in the invasion of Madagascar which kept the Japanese at bay early on in the war. The bravery displayed by the aircrew during the attacks on the *Bismarck* is legendary, while equal, but fruitless courage was exhibited during the ill-fated Channel Dash. The latter incident, in particular, not only says a lot about the aircraft, but also about the crews. They were under no illusion, being aware that the Swordfish was not the best aircraft they could have gone to war in but they would fight in to the death nevertheless. Regardless, it outlived its operational replacement, the Albacore by some years, mainly because the Swordfish was more suited to escort carrier and Mac-ship operations, a duty it carried out to the bitter end, protecting convoys far and wide.

Several members of 813 Squadron at Blida are told by the photographer, 'walk towards the camera, and look happy doing it'! From left to right our jolly subjects are: Sub Lt P C Heath, Sub Lt G A Donaghue, Sub Lt D R Mudd, Sub Lt R S Hankey (Senior Pilot), Sub Lt H O'Donnell, Lt Cdr C Hutchinson (CO), Sub Lt R D Pears, Sub Lt D Walker and 'unknown'. (*Aeroplane*)

Swordfish
Fairey's Successful Torpedo-Bomber

KEY
Books

HISTORIC MILITARY AIRCRAFT SERIES, VOLUME 28

Published by Key Books
An imprint of Key Publishing Ltd
PO Box 100
Stamford
Lincs PE9 1XQ

www.keypublishing.com

Original editions published as *Aeroplane Icons: Swordfish*
© 2013, edited by Martyn Chorlton

This edition © 2023

ISBN 978 1 80282 481 0

Typeset by SJmagic DESIGN SERVICES, India.

Chapter 1

The Fairey Swordfish Story

Fairey grows in strength

The year 1929 was big for Fairey, especially with regard to its value, which was strong enough to begin approaching outside shareholders. With assets valued at £615,486, the Fairey Aviation Company Limited was registered as a public company on March 5, 1929. The same year, Fairey was asked not

only to vacate their original factory at Clayton Road but also Northolt Aerodrome, from which it had been flight testing aircraft since 1917. It was a blessing in disguise for the latter, as Fairey was rapidly outgrowing the hangar space allocated for its use. Northolt's replacement was a 150-acre site at Harmondsworth in Middlesex, which was bought for £15,000. From the summer of 1930, Harmondsworth became Fairey's main flight test centre. It would remain so until 1944, when the site was requisitioned by the Air Ministry, despite plans to turn the airfield into another large extension of the Hayes factory. While concrete runways and massed expansion was carried out, the military never fully took over, instead the airfield evolved into Heathrow Airport.

Fairey were offered Heston as an alternative in early 1945 but this proved unsuitable because of air traffic control issues and instead the company opted for White Waltham, which was taken over in November 1947. Heston continued to serve as the point of

The Fairey T.S.R.II Torpedo Spotter Reconnaissance prototype, K4190, being put through its paces by Fairey test pilot Chris Staniland in the summer of 1934. (*Aeroplane*)

One of Fairey's greatest and possibly, most surprising success stories, the Fairey Swordfish. (*Aeroplane*)

departure for newly built aircraft, which were fully flight tested at White Waltham. Remarkably, the compensation that Fairey was owed for the Air Ministry's requisition of Harmondsworth was not fully settled until 1964, by which time the company had already moved on from aircraft manufacturing. Harmondsworth's 'billiard table' surface made it ideal for flight testing and the first prototype to make its maiden flight from here was the Hendon on November 25, 1930.

Enter the Swordfish, just!

Only those people who actually worked for Fairey and the many civil servants involved in the specification for the Fairey Swordfish ever knew how close the type came to being scrubbed. The loss of the TSR.I in September 1933, luckily for Fairey, took place eight months before the company's main competitor for the specification, the Blackburn Shark, first flew. The aircraft's replacement, the TSR.II was designed and manufactured in an incredibly short period of time. Cutting every conceivable works procedure, the components were manufactured wherever space could be found within the Hayes factory walls. In seven short months, the TSR.II prototype, later to be named Swordfish was completed but Fairey was left to wait until April 1935 when the first production order was placed.

When another large order for the Battle was received it was time to expand again and, in late 1935, Fairey took over the ex-Willys-Overland Crossley car factory at Heaton Chapel in Stockport. Hayes was expanded again on October 1938 when a brand new research department was opened by Air Minister, Sir Kingsley Wood. It was the country's first private venture research centre and the well-equipped facility included a large wind-tunnel, which had a test chamber 22ft long and a working section 12ft high and 10ft wide.

The vast Fairey 'empire'

By the beginning of the Second World War, Fairey were responsible for 25 factories and workshops of their own and many more that were operated by a host of sub-contractors of varying sizes. By now the Fairey Group was not only producing aircraft but also providing spares, aircraft repair, production and repair of propellers, production of standardised components for the aviation industry as a whole, production of special machinery and experimental work across the board.

New aircraft were built at Hayes and Heaton Chapel, which had satellite factories spread across the north-west. Aircraft were assembled and flight tested at Heathrow (ex-Harmondsworth) in the south and from Ringway in the north. The Swordfish, Albacore and Firefly were all built at Hayes, until Blackburn took over in 1940. At Heaton Chapel, the Battle, Fulmar and Barracuda poured out by the hundred while a shadow factory at Errwood Park carried out the sub-contract production of the Beaufighter and Halifax.

During the war years Charles Fairey was ordered to work for the British Air Commission in the US, an appointment he was criticised for accepting, despite having no choice at the time. However, in hindsight, Charles' work in the US was far more important than the future of his own company at the time. The problem with his departure across the pond in August 1940 was that Charles had not left anyone behind with complete control over the company and even up to this point he had devoted much of his time working for the Ministry of Aircraft Production (MAP) under the control of Lord Beaverbrook.

With Charles away, Fairey's aircraft production at Hayes inevitably did not run as smoothly as hoped. For example, pending the taking over of Swordfish production by Blackburn and frustratingly slow progress with Albacore production (in 1942 Hayes was brimming with Albacores when it should have been producing Fireflies), the Firefly was delayed by more than a year. It was a similar story at Heaton Chapel, where Barracuda production was delayed until 1942, although this was more due to the demand for the Rolls-Royce engine during the early part of the war.

The imposing main headquarters building of the Fairey Aircraft Company Limited at Hayes, during the late 1940s. (via Martyn Chorlton)

The sprawl of the main Fairey factory at Hayes, looking west as it appeared in June 1946. (Fairey Surveys via Martyn Chorlton)

The Fairey S.9/30, S1706, at Felixstowe in May 1936, during trials alongside Hawker Osprey III, S1700. (via Martyn Chorlton)

The S.9/30 & TSR.I: the Swordfish begins

It seems remarkable to think that an aircraft that was designed to one specification, led to another that was designed two specifications later; both machines making their maiden flights a mere eight weeks apart. That is what occurred with the S.9/30, which in turn evolved into the TSR.I and then the TSR.II; the latter also becoming known as the Swordfish.

S.9/30 LAND AND FLOATPLANE AND TSR.I

ENGINE	(S.9/30) one 525hp Rolls-Royce Kestrel IIMS; (TSR.I) one 625hp Armstrong Siddeley Panther VI and later one 635hp Bristol Pegasus IIM
WINGSPAN	(S.9/30 Land) 46ft; (folded) 17ft 10in
LENGTH	(land) 34ft 1in; (float) 39ft 3in
HEIGHT	(land) 14ft; (float) 16ft 6in
WING AREA	442 sq ft
LOADED WEIGHT	(land) 5,740lb; (float) 6,500lb
MAX SPEED	(land) 147mph at 2,000ft; (float) 136mph at 2,000ft
CLIMB	(land) 5,000ft in 5 min 30 sec; (float) 5,000ft in 6.3 min

The Marcel Lobelle designed S.9/30, was first flown as a landplane with a divided undercarriage and low-pressure tyres. (via Martyn Chorlton)

What actually occurred was that the Fairey designers were looking way beyond the original Specification S.9/30, which was issued in June 1930. By the time the aircraft flew in 1934, the requirement had predictably passed in favour of S.15/33 but Fairey had already been working on their TSR.I, which was intended for service with the Greek Navy. The TSR.I was then put forward as a contender for S.15/33, but despite being destroyed in a crash, the design was carried on with the TSR.II and the FAA went on to receive its greatest ever torpedo-bomber.

A two-bay biplane on the surface, the Fairey S.9/30 was actually a single: the inboard inter-plane struts were only there to provide rigidity for when the wings were folded. A de-rated Kestrel IIMS engine powered the S.9/30, an engine that used evaporative cooling via surface-type steam condensers attached to the lower side of the upper wing. The fuselage was made of stainless-steel strip and tube and was constructed in four sections.

The TSR.I was a privately financed project powered by a 625hp Panther radial engine and, despite being designed specifically for the Greek Navy, no orders were forthcoming. Prior to its bland designation name, the aircraft was referred to within the company walls as the 'Greek Machine'. Once the order fell through, the aircraft was re-engined with a 635hp Pegasus IIM engine cowled off with a Townend ring. The fixed undercarriage was trialled with and without spats; the rear fuselage was strengthened for deck operations and an arrestor hook was fitted.

The Fairey S.9/30 was first flown from Harmondsworth by Chris Staniland on February 22, 1934. Following its initial visit to the A&AEE, which was academic as the specification criteria had already been passed, the aircraft, serially S1706 was converted into a seaplane. Fitted with a large central float and smaller floats mounted on struts under the outer wings, S1706 was trialled at the MAEE, Felixstowe alongside the Hawker Osprey. The S.9/30 performed well, but the derivate of the all-conquering Hart family won the day and Osprey was chosen instead. S1706 was struck off charge on November 30, 1936 and ended its days being used for crash barrier trials.

The privately funded TSR.I fitted with a Bristol Pegasus engine inside a Townend ring, driving a Watts propeller. (*Aeroplane*)

The TSR.I, also referred to by its construction number, F.1875, powered by an Armstrong Siddeley Panther engine. (via Martyn Chorlton)

The TSR.1, which remained un-serialled, was first flown by Staniland on March 21, 1933 in its original Greek Navy form. Accepted as a contender for Specification S.15/33, trials were progressing well until September 11, 1933, when Staniland failed to recover from a flat spin and was forced to abandon the aircraft after twelve rotations. Regardless, flight reports showed that the aircraft was more than capable to meet the specification and all the knowledge and experienced gained was ploughed into the TSR.II

TSR.II & Swordfish I

As mentioned earlier, the roots of the TSR.II, which would be renamed in the Swordfish are firmly planted in the story of the S.9/30 and the TSR.I. Following the loss of the latter in September 1933, Marcel Lobelle immediately set to work re-designing the TSR.I to a new more advanced specification.

Air Ministry Specification S.15/33 was for a Naval carrier-borne torpedo/spotter/reconnaissance (TSR) aircraft, which was a more advanced version of S.9/30. On the surface, the second aircraft, the TSR.II, was very similar to the TSR.I, only differing in having an extra bay in the fuselage and spin recovery strakes ahead of the tailplane (a lesson learned from the loss of the TSR.I).

The prototype TSR (Torpedo/Spotter/Reconnaissance) Mk II (later Swordfish), K4190, first flew on April 17, 1934. After a host of trials, the aircraft settled with 'A' Flight/Station Flight at Gosport but, on June 23, 1938, the Swordfish overturned on landing because the brakes had been left on after a catapult take-off. The aircraft was SOC (Struck off Charge) eight weeks later. (*Aeroplane*)

The upper wing had a sweepback of 4° to compensate for the longer fuselage while other differences included a greater chord fin and rudder. Construction was generally similar to the TSR.I; the TSR.II having a pair of built-up steel-strip spars, duralumin ribs in the wings, steel drag struts and a steel-tube fuselage. Power was provided by a Pegasus IIM3 engine, cowled by substantial Townend-ring, driving a two-blade wooden Watts propeller, although later, a three-blade metal type became standard.

The TSR.II, serialled K4190, was first flown on April 17, 1934 by Chris Staniland and, two months later, was being trialled at Martlesham Heath, followed by the RAE for catapult trials, then on board HMS *Courageous* for deck landing tests.

Approximately 32,000 Pegasus engines were produced during the 1930s and 1940s to power tens of different aircraft, including the Swordfish, Sunderland and Wellington to name a few. (via Martyn Chorlton)

By April 1935, the TSR.II had been renamed the Swordfish and a pre-production order for three aircraft, then a production batch of 86 aircraft followed. The first pre-production aircraft, K5660, was first flown on December 31, 1935.

The Swordfish entered service in July 1936 when it joined 825 Squadron on board HMS *Glorious*, the unit having previously operated the IIIF. By the end of the year, three more FAA squadrons had re-equipped with the Swordfish and, by late 1938, three more had re-equipped; the majority of them having replaced Blackburn Sharks and Fairey Seals. This left the Swordfish as the FAA's only torpedo-bomber until the arrival of the Fairey Albacore in March 1940.

By the beginning of the Second World War, 13 operational FAA squadrons were equipped with the Swordfish and a further twelve would be formed during the conflict. On top of these, 25 operational squadrons and a further 22 second-line squadrons also operated the Swordfish and eleven catapult flights.

The Swordfish I served with great distinction in all theatres of the war but special mention should be made regarding the aircraft's involvement in the successful

SELF-DEFENCE

The Swordfish I was fitted with a fixed-forward firing .303in Vickers Mk 2 machine gun fed by a 600-round box-type magazine positioned on the starboard side of the aircraft in front of the pilot's cockpit. This weapon was removed from later production aircraft.

Rear defence was provided by a .303in Lewis or Vickers 'K' machine gun which was mounted on a Fairey High Speed Gun Mounting and operated by the TAG. Six 100-rpd (rounds per drum) magazines were located in the aft cockpit.

.303in Lewis

Total Length	40in
Barrel Length	20in
Weight (empty)	19lb 8oz
Magazine	100 rpd
Rate of fire	1,050 rpm
Velocity	2,450ft/sec

.303in Vickers 'K'

Total Length	50.5in
Barrel Length	26.25in
Weight (empty)	26lb
Magazine	47 or 97 rpd
Rate of fire	550 rpm
Velocity	2,450ft/sec

All Blackburn-built Swordfish were nicknamed 'Blackfish' by Fairey staff and Hayes, including this Mk II LS268 pictured at Boscombe Down. Built to contract B31192/39, this aircraft was from a batch of 250 which were delivered to the FAA from May 1943 onwards. (via Martyn Chorlton)

There is no hiding the large radome which houses the ASV Mk X of this Swordfish III pictured at Boscombe Down in July 1944. Three hundred and twenty Mk IIIs were built by Blackburn, many going on to serve in support of the Atlantic and Russian conveys, achieving several U-boat kills to their credit. (via Martyn Chorlton)

110 Swordfish IIs were modified with canopies over the cockpits for training in Canada. Referred to as the Mk IV, there is no actual official evidence from the period when this designation was used. (via Martyn Chorlton)

attack against Italian warships in Taranto harbour on November 11, 1940 and the demise of the *Bismarck* in May 1941.

The Swordfish I also served with RAF units, 8 and 202 Squadrons, between August and December 1940 and October 1940 and June 1941 respectively; the latter operating the seaplane variant.

The Swordfish outlived its operational replacement, the Albacore, by many years (mainly because of the larger aircraft's unsuitability to operate from escort carriers). It was whilst aboard MAC ships that the Swordfish carried out its last operational duty on May 21, 1945 with 836 Squadron.

A total of 992 Swordfish Mk Is were built; 692 of them by Fairey at Hayes, (201 of this number were delivered in 1937 alone) and 300 of them by Blackburn at Sherburn-in-Elmet.

TSR.II & SWORDFISH I

ENGINE	One 690hp Bristol Pegasus IIIM3 nine-cylinder radial
WINGSPAN	(TSR) 45ft 5in; (I) 45ft 6in
LENGTH	(TSR) 36ft 6in; (I) 35ft 8in
HEIGHT	(I) 12ft 4in
WING AREA	(TSR) 542 sq ft; (I) 607 sq ft
EMPTY WEIGHT	(I) 4,195lb
LOADED WEIGHT	(I) 7,720lb
MAX SPEED	(I) 154mph
CRUISING SPEED	(I) 131mph
SERVICE CEILING	(I) 19,250ft
DURATION	5.7 hr

Swordfish II & III (including IV)

The design of the Swordfish II, III and IV differed little from the Swordfish I. Introduced into production by Blackburn in 1941, the Mk II was the most prolifically built of all Swordfish. The most significant difference from the earlier mark was that from the Mk II onwards, the underside

of the lower wing was strengthened with a metal skin enabling the aircraft to carry up to eight 60lb RPs. It was this very effective, yet simple weapon that was tested by a Swordfish at the A&AEE during 1941 for the first time.

The original 690hp Pegasus powered many early Swordfish Mk IIs but this was later replaced by the 750hp Pegasus 30 which was installed in all later aircraft, including all Mk IIIs and Mk IVs.

The Swordfish III also had a strengthened lower wing but was additionally modified to carry an ASV (Air-to-Surface-Vessel) Mk X radar inside a large radome mounted between the undercarriage legs. The Swordfish IV was basically a Mk II fitted with a fully enclosed canopy specifically for training use in Canada.

Basic defensive armament was the same as the Swordfish I; all later marks could also carry a single 18in torpedo, a 1,500lb sea mine or the same weight in bombs and depth charges. Because of the strengthened

SWORDFISH II & III LANDPLANE

ENGINE	One 690hp Bristol Pegasus IIIM3 nine-cylinder radial and later one 750hp Pegasus 30.
WINGSPAN	45ft 6in
LENGTH	35ft 8in
HEIGHT	12ft 4in
WING AREA	607 sq ft
EMPTY WEIGHT	4,700lb
LOADED WEIGHT	6,750lb
MAX SPEED	(Torpedo bomber) 139mph at 4,750ft
CRUISING SPEED	104-129mph at 5,000ft
CLIMB RATE	(III) 5,000ft in 10 mins
RANGE	(Normal fuel & 1,610lb torpedo) 546 miles

FAIREY SWORDFISH PRODUCTION

Fairey-built

Fairey TSR.I prototype built to Specification S.15/33
No serial

Fairey Swordfish (TSR.II) prototype delivered in May 1934 by Fairey, Hayes to Contract 280480/33 and built to Specification 38/34 K4190

Three Fairey Swordfish Is delivered in January 1936 by Fairey, Hayes to Contract 402278/35 K5660-K5662

86 Fairey Swordfish Is delivered between February and August 1936 by Fairey, Hayes to Contract 402278/35 K5926-K6011

104 Fairey Swordfish Is delivered between October 1936 and April 1937 by Fairey, Hayes to Contract 466845/35 K8346-K8449

27 Fairey Swordfish Is delivered in April and May 1937 by Fairey, Hayes to Contract 466845/35 K8860-K8886

150 Fairey Swordfish Is delivered between June 1937 and January 1938 by Fairey, Hayes to Contract 534297/36 L2717-L2866

62 Fairey Swordfish Is delivered between February and June 1938 by Fairey, Hayes to Contract 672134/37 L7632-L7661 & L7670-L7701

60 Fairey Swordfish Is delivered between June and October 1938 by Fairey, Hayes to Contract 743308/38
L9714-L9743 & L9756-L9785

200 Fairey Swordfish Is delivered between January 1939 and February 1940 by Fairey, Hayes to Contract 963679/38
P3991-P4039, P4061-P4095, P4123-P4169, P4191-P4232 & P4253-P4279

Blackburn-built aka 'Blackfish'

300 Fairey Swordfish Is delivered between December 1940 and October 1941 by Blackburn, Sherburn-to-Elmet to Contract B.31192/39
V4288-V4337, V4360-V4399, V4411-V4455, V4481-V4525, V4551-V4600, V4621-V4655 & V4685-V4719

100 Fairey Swordfish Is delivered between October and December 1941 by Blackburn, Sherburn-in-Elmet to Contract B.31192/39 W5836-W5865, W5886-W5925 & W5966-W5995

100 Fairey Swordfish IIs delivered between December 1941 and April 1942 by Blackburn, Sherburn-in-Elmet to Contract B.31192/39 DK670-DK719 & DK743-DK792

400 Fairey Swordfish IIs delivered between May 1942 and May 1943 by Blackburn, Sherburn-in-Elmet to Contract B.31192/39 HS154-HS196, HS208-HS231, HS579-HS625 & HS637-HS678

250 Fairey Swordfish IIs delivered between May and October 1943 by Blackburn, Sherburn-in-Elmet to Contract B.31192/39 LS151-LS193, LS214-LS248, LS261-LS299, LS315-LS358, LS362-LS403 & LS415-LS461

230 Fairey Swordfish IIs delivered October 1943 and February 1944 by Blackburn, Sherburn-in-Elmet to Contract B.31192/39 NE858-NE906, NE920-NE957, NE970-NE999, NF113-NF161, NF175-NF217 & NF230-NF250

120 Fairey Swordfish IIIs delivered between February and August 1944 by Blackburn, Brough to Contract B.31192/39 NF251-NF274, NF298-NF347 & NF369-NF414

200 Fairey Swordfish IIIs delivered between May and August 1944* by Blackburn, Brough to Contract B.31192/39 NR857-NR898, NR913-NR958, NR970-NR999, NS112-NS156 & NS168-NS204

* The last six Swordfish built, NS199-NS204 were delivered to 813, 835, 836 Squadrons on August 18, 1944

400 Mk Is & Mk IIs cancelled in the following serial range: RL435-RL993
200 Mk IIIs cancelled in the following serial range: NS205-NS484

NS204, the last of 1,699 built by Blackburn at Sherburn-in-Elmet and Brough prepares to leave the former on August 18, 1944 bound for 813 Squadron. (via Martyn Chorlton)

wing, as well as the eight RPs, the Mk II and III could alternatively carry eight 25lb armour-piercing RPs on the same under-wing rails.

The Mk III also had the option of being fitted with rocket-assisted take-off gear (RATOG) designed for Swordfish operations with heavy loads from short decks, such as escort carriers and MAC (Merchant Air Carriers) ships. Several Swordfish were also modified to accept a Leigh light under the port wing for nocturnal submarine hunting.

The Swordfish II entered FAA service in 1941 and the Mk III in 1943, both continuing to serve until mid-1946. The Swordfish II served with a remarkable 64 FAA squadrons, 23 of them operational. The Swordfish Mk III served with 20 different FAA squadrons and between the two marks the type served at sea aboard HMS *Argus*, *Ark Royal*, *Courageous*, *Eagle*, *Furious*, *Glorious*, *Hermes*, *Illustrious*, *Indefatigable* and *Victorious*. The MAC ships and escort carriers including HMS *Activity*, *Archer*, *Attacker*, *Avenger*, *Battler*, *Biter*, *Campania*, *Chaser*, *Dasher*, *Fencer*, *Hunter*, *Nairana*, *Rapana*, *Stalker*, *Tracker* and *Vindex* were also frequented by Swordfish IIs and IIIs.

All production of the Swordfish II, III and the Mk IV conversions was carried out by the Blackburn Aircraft Company at Sherburn in Elmet, North Yorkshire. This equated to 1,080 Mk IIs and 320 Mk IIIs. One hundred and ten Mk IIs were converted to Mk IVs and Blackburn also supplied the Royal Canadian Navy with 99 Mk IIs and six Mk IIIs.

Chapter 2

The 'Stringbag' Joins the Fleet

Operational debut

It was 825 Squadron, under the command of Lt Cdr H A Traill, which was the first operational FAA unit to receive the Swordfish whilst ashore from HMS Glorious at Hal Far, Malta in July, 1936. The aircraft had been shipped out in June and re-assembled at Kalafrana and Hal Far under the close eye of Fairey representative, Mr C B Baker. Re-equipping from the Fairey IIIF began on July 28 and was completed on August 27.

Following a few days of preliminary flight training, which was an easy transition for crew who had flown the previous Fairey aircraft, all Swordfish and squadron personal boarded *Glorious* again on October 30 for deck-landing practice. Within ten days 825 Squadron was back ashore at Hal Far and on January 4, 1937 the squadron's work-up on the Swordfish was complete and *Glorious* embarked on a 'Spring Cruise'.

It was not long before the first serious accident occurred and on February 5, as the Mediterranean Fleet was approaching Alexandria, K5938 '971' and K5947 '978' collided in mid-air at a height of just

One of 825 Squadron's first aircraft was K5945 '975' which was delivered via Gosport in April 1936, PD Sealand in early July and onto Malta, arriving on unit strength on July 27, 1936. (via Owen Cooper)

Although the prototype, K4190 did not enter operational service, it paved the way for the hundreds of production aircraft that did and the trials it carried out, especially on floats as depicted here, proved invaluable for the Swordfish when it joined the Fleet as a catapult seaplane. (*Aeroplane*)

With its main engine cowling removed, P3992 'G5K' of 825 Squadron has its Pegasus engine tested, most likely following an overhaul, on board HMS *Glorious* in 1939. (via Owen Cooper)

150ft and crashed into the sea. The crew of '978', Lt G A Vardon and TAG B Overal drowned following their ditching while Lt G C Newcombe and his unnamed TAG in '971' were rescued.

HMS *Glorious* returned to Malta again on March 23 but one month later, set sail for home so that its aircraft could participate in the forthcoming Coronation Review Flypast. On May 5, 825 Squadron disembarked to Gosport from where, on May 20, the unit flew with the might of the FAA for His Majesty King George VI. On June 23, 825 Squadron were back on board *Glorious* destined to spend the following two years serving in the Mediterranean, the only difference being that the unit's shore base was changed from Hal Far to Dekheila from May 1939.

The arrival of the multi-purpose Swordfish came at the right time for the Fleet TSR squadrons, which were operating a motley group of Fairey IIIF and Seals and Blackburn Baffins and Sharks. The latter in particular would not be missed as their Armstrong Siddeley Tiger engines had been nothing but trouble.

Ever increasing numbers

811 Squadron, under the command of Lt Cdr L I G Richardson, were the next unit to re-equip from the Baffin to the Swordfish in October 1936. Operating from HMS *Furious*, 811 Squadron was the first unit of the Home Fleet to convert. HMS *Glorious* became an all-Swordfish affair from November 9, 1936 when 823 Squadron, under the command of Lt Cdr G C Dickens, gave up their Seals. Operating from HMS *Eagle* (also on patrol in the Mediterranean), 812 Squadron was next when it replaced its Baffin's with Swordfish from December 7.

The year 1937 would see all operational TSR squadrons re-equipped with the Swordfish beginning in February, when nine Swordfish became the nucleus of a new 824 Squadron, which boarded HMS *Eagle* at Portsmouth. Three months later the ship reached the China Station where the old 824 Squadron, operating Seals from HMS *Hermes* and the shore base at Kai Tak was replaced by the Swordfish. HMS *Eagle* was also carrying nine Swordfish of 813 Squadron which had formed at Gosport on January 18, 1937, under the command of Lt Cdr C R V Pugh.

Pre-war strength achieved

The year 1937 would also see the demise of three Shark units operating from HMS *Courageous*, namely 810, 820 and 821, which all converted to Swordfish, and 822 Squadron on board *Furious*. HMS *Furious* was paid off in 1938 pending a full refit and its squadrons were transferred to *Courageous* for deck-landing training duties pending the entry into service of the purpose-built aircraft carrier, HMS *Ark Royal*. 814 Squadron was formed with Swordfish in December 1938 for HMS *Ark Royal*, joining it on January 11, 1939 while 811 and 822 Squadrons had their identities removed to become 767 (Deck Landing Training) Squadron, which was formed at Donibristle on May 24, 1939. On this day the Royal Navy finally re-gained control of their aviation component which was lost when the RNAS was dissolved to become part of the RAF on April 1, 1918. All aircraft being operated by the FAA were

Looking considerably worse for wear is K5934 of 825 Squadron after landing a tad too fast and overrunning onto the lower flying deck on March 8, 1939. The crew were unhurt and the aircraft was later repaired to serve with 3 AACU and 842 Squadron until February 1942. (*Aeroplane*)

811 Squadron was the second front-line FAA unit to receive the Swordfish from October 1936 in place of the Blackburn Baffin, which was fully retired the following month. K8440 is pictured on HMS *Furious*, a carrier that the unit operated from, on and off, until January 1939 when 811 Squadron joined HMS *Courageous*. This association came to abrupt end on September 17, 1939 when the carrier was sunk by a U-boat. (*Aeroplane*)

HMS *Glorious* gained a second Swordfish unit from November 1936 when 823 Squadron gave up its Seals. K5969 '803' carries out deck-landing practice aboard *Glorious* somewhere in the Mediterranean. Following a sortie out of Hal Far on April 20, 1938, the Swordfish ran out of fuel and was forced to ditch alongside the battleship HMS *Warspite*; both crew were rescued. (via Owen Cooper)

now under Admiralty charge and as a result, several new second-line units, at first numbered from 750 onwards were formed; many of them would later be equipped with the Swordfish.

Catapult

The Swordfish also had an important role as a catapult seaplane operating from large warships only, because of the aircraft's size. The task of providing the Royal Navy with these aircraft was in the hands of 701 and 705 (Catapult) Flights which provided and operated Swordfish from the 1st Battle Squadron and Battle Cruiser Squadron which operated, generally, in the Mediterranean. Originally designated as 444 Flight, 701 Flight was formed on July 15, 1936 at Kalafrana under the command of Lt Cdr A C G Ermen during a re-organisation of catapult units. A pair of Swordfish catapult seaplanes had already arrived with 444 Flight when it was operating from Mount Batten. These two aircraft joined the battle cruiser HMS *Repulse*.

The entry into service for the Swordfish seaplane was not without its problems, which concerned the water rudders. These were linked directly to the aircraft's own rudder controls, and during their development the floats' rudders had increased in size to give them sufficient response whilst taxiing on the water. However, this had the knock-on problem of affecting the aircraft's aerodynamics in flight. While HMS *Repulse* was being prepared to embark for a Fleet exercise, a group of engineers worked on the two Swordfish by installing a de-clutching system which could disconnect the water rudders whilst the aircraft was in flight. Only minutes before *Repulse* left Portsmouth, the modification was done and was later carried out on all other Swordfish seaplanes.

A pair of catapult-launched Swordfish seaplanes were also installed aboard HMS *Barham*, *Malaya*, *Resolution*, *Valiant* and *Warspite*. The 33,000-ton battleship HMS *Malaya* bucked the

One of four 812 Squadron Swordfish seaplanes, K5950 '62', being lifted aboard HMS *Glorious* in July 1937. The four aircraft, including K5950, were later transferred to HMS *Malaya* to operate under the banner of 701 (Catapult) Flight from September 1939 to July 1938. (via Owen Cooper)

The full complement of twelve Swordfish Is of 823 Squadron pictured over their carrier, HMS *Glorious*, possibly taken during the Coronation Review Flypast off Spithead on May 20, 1937. (via Owen Cooper)

BEWARE OF

Two pre-war Swordfish Is were allocated the 820 Squadron code 'A4B' whilst operating from HMS *Ark Royal.* This machine could either be L2787 or L9781; both gave the squadron good service. (via Owen Cooper)

Above: Swordfish of 821 Squadron in the foreground and 820 Squadron towards the stern prepare for take-off from HMS *Ark Royal* during the summer of 1939. Only L9780 '682' can be clearly identified (front left), and served with 821 Squadron from just April to July 1939. The aircraft enjoyed a long trouble-free career and was still going strong, flying out of Arbroath on June 1945. (via Owen Cooper)

Left: 823 Squadron pictured over the Royal Yacht, from where King George VI is taking the salute during the Coronation Review Flypast on May 20, 1937. (*Aeroplane*)

trend when it took on four Swordfish seaplanes from 'B' Flight of 812 Squadron, originally operating from HMS *Glorious*, on September 15, 1937. These were taken on board whilst the ship was docked at Mudros for a period of six months before the complement was reduced to a pair of Swordfish in March 1938.

Off to war we go

When war broke out on September 3, 1939, the FAA had eleven operational units equipped with the Swordfish: 810, 811, 812, 813, 814, 820, 821, 822, 823, 824 and 825, plus 767 Squadron, 701 and 705, which by then had been upgraded to full squadron status. This number had been bolstered by the formation of 818 Squadron at Evanton on August 24, 1939 and originally intended to form at

SWORDFISH UNITS JULY 1936–SEP 1939

701 Sqn	I/SP	Sep 1936 at Kalafrana
702 Sqn	I/SP	1939 at Lee-on-Solent
705 Sqn	I/SP	Jul 1936 at Kalafrana
765 Sqn	I/SP	May 1939 at Lee-on-Solent
767 Sqn	I	May 1939 at Donibristle & HMS *Furious*
771 Sqn		May 1939 at Portland
810 Sqn	I	Sep 1937 at Gosport, Evanton, HMS *Courageous*, Southampton, Roborough, Old Sarum, HMS *Ark Royal*, Dekheila, Aboukir, Lee-on-Solent & Warmwell
811 Sqn	I	Oct 1936 at Donibristle, HMS *Furious*, Gosport, Aboukir, Evanton & Lee-on-Solent; Redesignated 767 Sqn on May 24, 1939
812 Sqn	I	Dec 1936 at Hal Far, HMS *Glorious*, Gosport, HMS *Courageous* & Dekheila
813 Sqn	I	Jan 1937 at Gosport, HMS *Eagle*, Hal Far, Seletar, Kai Tak, Wei-Hai-Wei (det) & Penang
814 Sqn	I	Dec 1938 at Southampton, HMS *Ark Royal*, Warmwell, Worthy Down & Roborough
818 Sqn	I	Aug 1939 at Evanton & HMS *Ark Royal*
820 Sqn	I	Sep 1937 at Southampton, HMS *Courageous*, Evanton, Eastleigh, Southampton, HMS *Ark Royal*, Half Far (det), Lee-on-Solent, Gosport, Ford and Donibristle
821 Sqn	I	Sep 1937 at Lee-on-Solent (det), Evanton (det), Gosport, Southampton, Portland (det), HMS *Courageous*, Eastchurch, HMS *Ark Royal* and Dekheila (det)
822 Sqn	I	Aug 1937 to May 1939 at Gosport, HMS *Furious*, Evanton (det), Gosport, Manston, Donibristle and HMS *Courageous* when unit absorbed into 767 Sqn in May 1939 May 1939 at Southampton, Donibristle and HMS *Courageous*
823 Sqn	I	Nov 1936 at Hal Far, HMS *Glorious*, Gosport, Aboukir and Dekheila
824 Sqn	I	Apr 1937 at Seletar, HMS *Eagle*, Kai Tak and Penang (det)
825 Sqn	I	Jul 1936 at Hal Far, HMS *Glorious*, Gosport, Abingdon, Southampton, Aboukir (det) and Dekheila (det)

Lee-on-Solent on October 11, imminent approach of the war brought this plan forward. Equipped with nine Swordfish, 818 Squadron, under the command of Lt Cdr J E Fenton (who took over on August 30), was hurriedly embarked on HMS *Ark Royal* anchored in Scapa Flow, which set sail for Norwegian waters on August 31.

By the beginning of the Second World War, the Swordfish had built up a well-deserved reputation for being a reliable and sturdy aircraft to operate. However, many thought the aircraft was already past its best and to point, they were correct, but the Swordfish was yet to prove itself in battle and when its day came, all of its critics kept their mouths shut. While more modern aircraft came and went, the Swordfish stoically remained an operational aircraft from the beginning of the war to the very end; a position very few other military aircraft could match.

UNIT CODES AND SERIALS FOR PRE-WAR 'FRONT-LINE' SWORDFISH UNITS

444 Sqn 1st Battle Sqn; codes accounted for (2 a/c 3.36-7.36)
'092' K5931 (3.36-7.36); '093' K5930 (3.36-7.36); K5926 (5.36-7.36) (code unknown)

701 Sqn 1st Battle Sqn; codes accounted for (4/5 a/c 9.37-5.39)
'72'; '075' K5957 (9.37-10.37); '73' K5959 (10.37-12.37), K8446 (2.39-5.39); K5930 (1938), '076'
K5950 (9.37-2.38); K8363 (9.38-1.39); '74' K8351 (9.37-11.37) & K8364 (12.38-5.39)
Serials for which codes not yet found: L2751 (11.38-5.39); L9767 (12.38-5.39) & L9766 (12.38-1.39)

702 Sqn 1st Battle Sqn (1 a/c 1.39-5.39)
Serial for which codes not yet found: L7670 (1.39-5.39)

705 Sqn 2nd Battle Sqn; codes accounted for (4/5 a/c 9.37-5.39)
'089'; '092' K5931 (7.36-1.38); '091' & '093' K5954 (9.36-1.38)
Serials for which codes not yet found: K5926 (from 7.36); K5948 (9.38); K5930 (from 9.36) &
L7687 (3.39)

810 Sqn HMS *Courageous*; codes accounted for (12 a/c 8.37-5.39)
'523' L2737 (9.37-7.38); '524' L2738 (9.37-8.38); '526' L2739 (9.37-5.39); '527' L2740 (8.37) &
K8434 (c.1937); '528' L2741 (9.37-1.38) & L2752 (5.38-1.39); '529' L2742 (12.37-4.38) & L2753
(5.38-3.39); '530' L2743 (9.37-3.39); '531' L2744 (9.37-3.39); '532' L2745 (9.37-5.38) & K8439
(5.38-8.38) & L7682 (8.38-5.39); '534' L2746 (from 9.37) & K8441 (5.38) & L2757 (5.38-5.39);
'536' L2748 (9.37-4.39) & L2747 (4.39-5.39); '537' K8435 (9.37-6.38) & L2828 (6.38-8.38) &
L7683 (8.38-9.38)
Serials for which codes not yet found: K5977 (to 5.38); L2756 (5.38); K8883 (4.39-5.39); L2767
(from 7.37); L2735 (4.39-5.39); L7684 (8.38); L2745 (9.38); L7685 (8.38); L2755 (c. 1937/8) &
L7694 (11.38-2.39)

811 Sqn HMS *Furious*; codes accounted for (12 a/c 10.36-5.39)
'601' K8357 (10.36-6.38); '602' K8367 (10.36-12.37) & K6006 (1.38-8.38); '603' K6003 (10.36-
3.38); '604' K8359 (11.36-5.39); '605' K8373 (11.36-2.38); 607?; '608' K8375 (11.36-3.37) & K8376
(37-7.38); '609' K8358 (10.36-7.38) & K8440 (1.39-5.39); '610' K8375 (37-8.38) & K8437 (3.37-
3.38) & L2761 (7.38-3.39); '612' K8366 (10.36-7.37) & K8374 (37-2.38); '613' K8368 (11.36-3.38)
& K8376 (3.37) & K8356 (1.39-3.39) & '614' K8376 (37-7.38)
Serials for which codes not yet found: K6004 (c. 1938); K6008 (8.37-12.37); K8371 (1.39);
K8372 (11.36-3.38); K8377 (11.36-5.38); K8378 (11.36-5.37); K8379 (11.36-8.37); K8433 (from
3.37); K8434 (from 3.37); K8435 (from 3.37); K8436 (from 3.37); K8438 (from 3.37); K8439
(3.37-3.38 & 1.39-5.39); K8440 (from 3.37); K8441 (3.37-4.38); L2719 (1.39-5.39); L2741 (5.38 &
1.39-5.39); L2746 (1.39-5.39); L2752 (1.39); L2754 (2.39); L2758 (7.38-3.39); L2759 (6.38-5.39);
L2762 (1.39-5.39); L2774 (11.38-5.39); L2775 (1.39-5.39) & L2776 (10.38-5.39)

812 Sqn HMS *Glorious*; codes accounted for (12 a/c 12.36-5.39) '60' K5960 (4.38-5.38); '61';
'62' K5950 (8.37); '63' K5950 (7.37-8.37) & K8443 (8.38-12.38) & L9762 (3.39-5.39); '64' K5952

(11.37-3.38) & K8383 (11.38); '65' K5978 (5.37-7.38) & K8371 (2.39-5.39); '70' K5957 (4.37-5.37)
& K8870 (1.38) & K5982 (4.38-5.38) & K5945 (4.39-5.39); '71' K5982 (7.37-8.37) & K5975 (3.38)
& K8447 (11.38) & K8868 (9.38-5.39); '72' K5957 (7.37-9.37 & 1.38-12.38) & L5932 (1.39-4.39);
'73' K8365 (11.36-9.37) & K5932 (1.37-4.39) & K8863 (12.38-5.39); '74' K5979 (3.37-10.37) &
K8352 (7.38-5.39); '75' K5975 (7.37-8.37) & K5982 (5.37 & 10.37) & K8447 (7.38) & K8870 (4.38-
7.38); '81' K5975 (7.37) & K5982 (c.1938)
Serials for which codes not yet found: K5935 (8.37-9.37); K5953 (3.37-11.38); K5976 (2.37); K5977
(2.37-6.37); K8351 (11.36-8.37); K8360 (11.36-5.39); K8361 (from 12.36); K8362 (from 12.36);
K8363 (from 11.36); K8369 (from 12.36); K8371 (from 11.36 & 12.37-1.38) & K8380 (2.39-5.39)

813 Sqn HMS *Eagle*; codes accounted for (9 a/c 1.37-5.39) '580' K8402 (1.37-5.39); '581' K8397
(1.37-5.39);'582' K8395 (1.37-5.39); '583' K8399 (1.37-5.39); '584' K5990 (11.37-4.38); '586'
K8400 (1.37-5.39); '587' K8396 (1.37-5.39); '589' K8398 (1.37-5.39) '590' K8401 (1.37-5.39)
Serials for which codes not yet found: K8417 (4.39-5.39)

814 Sqn HMS *Ark Royal*; codes accounted for (6 later 9 a/c 12.38-5.39) '701' L9777 (12.38-5.39);
'702' L9779 (12.38-5.39); '703' L2827 (12.38-4.39) & L2733 (4.39-5.39); 704' L9778 (12.38-5.39);
'705' L9775 (12.38-5.39); '706' L9768 (4.39-5.39); '708' L9774 (12.38-5.39); '709' L9773 (12.38-
5.39) & '710' L2764 (early 1939-5.39)
Serials for which codes not yet found: L2721 (11.38-12.38); L2736 (1.39-12.39) & L9782 (12.38-1.39)

820 Sqn HMS *Courageous*; codes accounted for (12 a/c 9.37-5.39) '645' K8879 (9.37-10.37)
& L7671 (8.38); '647' K8881 (9.37-2.39) & L2731 (4.39-5.39); '648' K8880 (9.37-2.39) & L2770
(8.38-1.39); '649' K8449 (9.37-3.38) & K5942 (5.38-8.38) & L7672 (9.38-5.39); '650' L9772 (10.38-
5.39) & L9781 (1.39-5.39); '651' K8861 (9.37-2.38); '652' K8882 (9.37-1.38) & L2718 (6.38); '653'
K8883 (9.37-11.38); '654'; '657' K8356 (6.38) & L7695 (11.38-4.39); '658' K8860 (9.37-10.38) &
L2732 (2.39) & '659' L2718 (to 10.38)
Serials for which codes not yet found: K8862 (9.37-5.38); K8864 (9.37-10.37); L2720 (9.37-
8.38); L2730 (11.38-4.39); L2760 (7.38-8.38 & 4.39); L2769 (9.38-5.39); L2771 (9.38-12.38) &
L7676 (9.38-5.39)

821 Sqn HMS *Courageous*/HMS *Ark Royal*; codes accounted for (9 a/c 9.37-5.39) '678'
K6000 (10.38-3.39); '679' L2723 (9.37-9.38); '680' L2720 (2.39-5.39); '681'; '682' L2765
(8.38-10.38) & L9780 (4.39-5.39); '683' L7675 (10.38-5.39); '684' L2731 (9.37-7.38) & L2768
(8.38-5.39); '685' L2732 (9.37-7.38) & K8879 (1.39-4.39); '687' L2733 (9.37-11.38) & '689'
L7673 (9.38-5.39)
Serials for which codes not yet found: K6006 (9.37-12.37); K6010 (1.38); K8367 (to 5.39); K8433
(1937/8); K8434 (9.38-4.39); K8882 (to 5.38); L2719 (9.37-11.37); L2721 (8.38-11.38); L2724
(9.37-11.38); L2725 (9.37-88.38); L2726 (8.37-7.38); L2730 (9.37); L2734 (9.37-7.38); L2735
(9.37-7.38); L2736 (9.37-6.38); L2760 (1.39); L2764 (8.38); L2766 '68x' (6.38-11.38); L2767 (8.38-
5.39); L7674 (3.38-9.38) & L9768 (2.39)

822 Sqn HMS *Furious*; codes accounted for (12 a/c 8.37-5.39) '901' K6011 (8.37-9.38); '902';
'903'; '904'; '905'; '906'; '907'; '910' & '912' K6009 (8.37-3.39)

Serials for which codes not yet found: K5989 (8.37-5.39); K5997 (9.38-2.39); K6000 (10.37-5.38); K6004 (8.37-5.38); K6005 (8.37-5.39); K6008 (10.37-5.39); K6010 (8.37-10.37 & 2.38-6.38); K8367 (2.38-3.38); K8379 (8.37-2.39); K8436 (10.37-7.38); L2737 (2.39-5.39); L2755 (6.38-3.39); L2756 (6.38-3.39); L2759 (8.37); L2760 (8.37); L2761 (8.37); L2753 (3.39); L2790 (c.1938); L2797 (c.1938); L2802 (c.1938); L2807 (c.1938); L2811 (c.1938) &L2814 (c.1938)

823 Sqn HMS *Glorious*; codes accounted for (12 a/c 11.36-5.39) '801' K5968 (11.36-4.39); '802' K5960 (11.36-2.38) & L9764 (to 5.39); '803' K5969 (11.36-4.38) & K8370 (4.38-5.39); '804' K5972 (11.36-5.39); '805' K5955 (11.36-11.38); '806' K5973 (11.36-8.37) & K5979 (9.36-1.37); '807' K5974 (11.36-6.37) & K8378 (10.37-5.39); '809' K5971 (11.36-2.37) & K5959 (7.37-2.39); '810' K8351 (8.37-1.39); '812' K5961 (11.36-5.39); '813' K5967 (11.36-5.39); '814' K5970 (11.36-5.38) & K5978 (from 11.36) & K8442 (12.38-3.39)
Serials for which codes not yet found: K5945 (10.38-3.39); K5950 (7.38-4.39); K5973 (11.38); K5975 (11.36); K5976 (11.36); K5977 (11.36); K5979 (1.39); K5980 (9.36-1.37); K5981 (from 9.36 & from 10.38); K5982 (from 9.36); K8383 (3.39) & L9763 (4.39-5.39)

824 Sqn HMS *Eagle*; codes accounted for (9 a/c 1.37-5.39) '945' K8386 (1.37-5.39); '946' K8390 (1.37-5.39); '947' K8392 (1.37-5.39); '948' K8387 (1.37-1.38) & K8409 (2.38-5.39); '950' K8388 (1.37-1.38) & K8406 (1.38-5.39); '951' K8389 (1.37-5.39); '952' K8391 (1.37-11.37) & K8414 (12.37-5.39); '953' K8393 (1.37-5.39) & '954' K8394 (1.37-5.39)

825 Sqn HMS *Glorious*; codes accounted for (12 a/c 7.36-5.39) '967' K5937 (7.36-2.39); '968' K5942 (7.36-6.37) & K8869 (6.37-10.38); '970' K5940 (7.36-7.38); '971' K5938 (7.36-2.37) & K8385 (5.39); '972' K5939 (7.36-10.38); '973' K5943 (7.36-8.37); '974' K5944 (7.36-5.38) & K8381 (7.38-10.39); '975' K5945 (7.36-10.38); '976' K5946 (7.36-5.39) & '978' K5947 (7.36-2.37) & K5936 (7.36-5.39) & K5976 (4.37-1.39); '980' K5948 (7.36-1.37) & K5980 (2.37-5.39) & '981' K5949 (7.36-3.39)
Serials for which codes not yet found: K5932 (3.39-5.39); K5933 ((7.36-1.39); K5934 (7.36-3.39); K5935 (7.36-5.37); K5851 (8.36-5.39); K5952 (8.36); K5955 (5.39-6.39); K5957 (from 8.36); K5973 (12.37 & 3.39-5.39); K5981 (4.37-8.37); K8354 (7.37-1.39); K8361 (12.37-10.38); K8381 (3.37-6.38); K8432 (10.38-4.39) & L9765 (2.39-5.39)

Chapter 3

Training Carrier

'A day or two in the life of HMS *Courageous* in March 1939' from *Flight*, March 9, 1939.

Grey mysteries of Rosyth

This is an eventful period in the development of British Naval Aviation. The Fleet Air Arm (soon to become the Naval Air Branch) is at a transitory stage, passing from the administration of the Air Ministry to that of the Admiralty. Complete control of the training of personnel is likely to be taken over on April 1, 1939.

Meanwhile there is tremendous activity in the production of specialised Fleet aircraft, carrier vessels and, of more immediate interest, pilots.

At such a time, therefore, Flight considers itself fortunate in having been represented on board HMS *Courageous* at the commencement of her current training programme in the North Sea.

We found the drifter Halo and tender to Courageous and among the grey mysteries of Rosyth Dockyard. She was nestling against a jetty, from the heights of which we contemplated the descent to her homely deck. Up on the bridge with the officer in command (a Fleet Air Arm pilot, by the way) we shunted and churned our way out into the darkening Firth of Forth with an exquisite train of seagulls, their wings golden from our lights, undulating over our wake.

The Forth Bridge soared above us and a toy train threaded its way through the triangulated girders as we nosed our way out through the boom defences.

Courageous, having stayed out to sea rather longer than anticipated, was late at our rendezvous in Aberlady Bay and for nearly an hour we thumped farther and farther toward the open sea, the Sub Lieutenant alternating between chart and binoculars.

Weighing in at 26,990 tons, HMS *Courageous* was 786ft 9in long of which 550ft of its length was taken up by a capacious, two-story hanger which could hold up to 48 Swordfish-sized aircraft. (via Owen Cooper)

The handling party rushes out to a Swordfish I, L2759 '602', which has just been brought to an abrupt halt by the first of four arrestor cables. Within minutes the aircraft is turned around, engine still running in preparation for another take-off. (*Aeroplane*)

A deck officer drops his flag indicating to the deck party to remove the chocks and pilot to open the throttle. (*Aeroplane*)

K8440 takes the cable aboard HMS *Courageous* in early 1939. The Swordfish I first joined 811 Squadron on HMS *Furious* in March 1937 before joining 811 Squadron and was coded '609', as depicted here. (*Aeroplane*)

Then we spotted her, far away in the blackness. Just faint rows of lights which, as we drew nearer, revealed her vast bulk, her boats and guns, booms and chains, brass-work and Carley floats and a group of figures in the stern, where we drew alongside, staring in wonder at the towering grey steelwork above.

A warm naval welcome

Then we met that hospitality which can only be described as Naval, being characterised not only by its friendliness but by its uncompromising welcome into an aura of supreme tradition. We were shepherded down a corridor leading from the quarter deck past racks of revolvers and rifles, white steel walls, shining brass-work and dark wood into the community which is an aircraft carrier.

Capt M L Clarke received us in his cabin and we were later introduced to Wg Cdr Jack Noakes, Lt Cdr E O F Price (OC 811 (TSR) Squadron, which operates as a training unit), and others whose job is to keep *Courageous* slipping through the water and the Swordfish flying from her deck.

'Eight eleven' was functioning early next morning and we soon left the wardroom for the windswept flying deck, a great expanse of steel flanked by safety palisades. Bracing ourselves against a 30-knot wind we attained the superstructure on the starboard side. Here are installed the Captain, officer of the watch, navigator, signals officer, Wg Cdr Noakes and Lt Cdr Price.

With Lt Cdr Price we shared 'The Kings Hut,' a pleasant little wooden structure round the rear of the funnel. This was built originally for the use of His Majesty King George V and now serves as a very useful vantage point from which the CO may survey the landings and take-offs of his trainees.

Incidentally, it is considered a heinous offence to refer to these as pupils; a number of the pilots practising landings on the day in question had nearly 600 hours in their log books. But no matter how masterly his handling of a Blenheim or a Hurricane, a pilot still requires the guidance of Lt Cdr Price and his flight commanders in learning the technique of deck landing, for it is quite a specialised business though not so difficult as it looks.

Originally captioned 'Pilots waiting in the palisades', these trainee pilots look on as one of their colleagues lands his Swordfish on HMS *Courageous*. The two pilots nearest the camera are the first of this group of ratings to land solo on the carrier. The less apprehensive of group, nearest the camera, is PO Fred Rice who would later win the DSC for his part in the sinking of U-64, the first U-boat to be sunk in the Second World War by an aircraft on April 13, 1940. (*Flight/Aeroplane*)

First solos

Confirmation was forthcoming from two rating pilots whom we were in time to watch making their first solo landings on the deck of an aircraft carrier. These two, unlike the ex-RAF personnel, had not taken the TSR course at Gosport, but were attached for deck landing training from 1 FTS, Netheravon. Although ranking as leading seamen, they were shortly to become petty officers.

While we were watching the trainees making their circuits Lt Cdr Price outlined for us the training programme. The whole of the flying personnel of his squadron is based at Donibristle, only the training staff (squadron commander, two flight commanders and the adjutant), a small batch of pilots together with four Fairey Swordfish torpedo-spotter-reconnaissance biplanes and two De Havilland Gipsy Moths, bring taken out in the *Courageous* on each trip. All the pilots, except the leading seamen, had turned over from the RAF and had already taken the TSR course at Gosport. With 811 Squadron they were being given not only deck landing training but a short syllabus dealing with the work of a first-line TSR squadron, including the tactics of the torpedo attack, reconnaissance exercises against a destroyer from Rosyth, and bombing of the high-level and diving varieties.

It is usual, if there are any battleships in the area, for the pilots to be shown a full-calibre 'shoot.' A new batch of about twelve pilots is received by the squadron every six weeks.

L2759 of 811 Squadron climbs away from HMS *Courageous* during a deck landing training course. The aircraft later served with 767 Squadron and 812 Squadron at North Coates, where it was lost in a mid-air collision with P4161 on July 20, 1940. (*Aeroplane*)

Sadly, there was no happy ending for HMS *Courageous*, which became the first British warship to be lost during the Second World War. It was sunk by U-29 on September 17, 1939 with the loss of 519 crew and all 24 Swordfish of 811 and 822 Squadrons.

On joining the *Courageous* the pilots under instruction do three landings in a Gipsy Moth, or, more accurately, the instructor does the first, the controls being handed over to the trainee for the second and third. If the instructor is satisfied that the pilot under instruction is competent he is transferred to a Swordfish and does three 'dummy runs' without landing before making a touch-down. In all, the pilots do about thirty landings during their week at sea, finishing with a landing with a passenger, one without the arrester wires and one with the Swordfish carrying a torpedo. When not practising landing on, the pilots are taken round the ship and are given lectures by the officers on aspects of naval life.

All training landings are directly controlled by one of the flight commanders who, stationed on the aft end of the flight deck, wields a pair of white wooden hand discs. Raising the discs above the head signifies that the pilot should go higher; dropping them below shoulder height, that he should come lower; and holding them in the form of a cross, that he should cut the engine. Farther up the deck is a second officer who, by means of hand flags, can acquaint a pilot of the fact that he has missed the arrester wires and that he must open up and make another circuit.

Total control

The machines are handled on the deck by the flight-deck party, composed of seamen from the ship's complement who work in four watches of twenty each. They are under the control of an officer who is responsible for the ranging of the aircraft and while flying is in progress betake themselves to the palisades.

There is a practical system of signals with coloured flags run out athwart the deck and by a mechanical shutter at the rear of the funnel. The shutter is used to signal the 'affirmative' for landing on. A green flag athwartships tells the pilot that his arrester hook is not lowered, while a red flag signifies that there is a hitch (as likely as not a failure in raising the arrester wires) and that he must not land his machine on until instructed. All these signals are under the control of the Wing Commander, who usually fires a Very light simultaneously with the showing of red or green flag.

Projecting from the port side of the ship toward the stern are booms which show the squadron pennant, denote by means of a flag what type of aircraft is operating from the deck and exhibit the 'dummy run' flag in the preliminary stages of training.

Incidentally, the Lieutenant Commander pointed out that the coloured band round the fuselage of a naval machine indicates to which carrier the aircraft belongs; blue, for example, represents the *Courageous*, and red the *Furious*.

Every landing and take-off is watched by Lt Cdr Price, who sets down his comments in a notebook while his recorder keeps check on other operational data. The record at the end of even a winter's day frequently shows between 120 and 140 landings.

Steep learning curve

One can stand hour after hour watching the flying and never become bored, particularly when an expert is at hand to point out, for instance, that a short pilot usually tends to look over the side of his cockpit while landing-on and in consequence, will drop a wing on the side in question. Even more striking than these little personal idiosyncrasies is the startling improvement which is always apparent after a few landings. There are, of course, difficulties which are not always eradicated so easily, notably the tendency to bounce the machine on the rounded-down end of the deck when landing-on and frequently at the cost of a fractured tail wheel.

One thing is certain. When these pilots under instruction go back to 'Doni-Bee', after a few days in *Courageous*, they are well on the way to becoming first-class deck-landing specialists.

Of the *Courageous*, we have already published a good deal of descriptive matter. There are, however, certain features which impress particularly. Prominent among these is the effectiveness of the deck arrester gear. This takes the form of stout steel wires running athwartships near the stern and raised above the deck on collapsible supports. Before landing-on the pilot of the aircraft lowers a hook beneath the fuselage of his machine, and this catches a wire. The shock is taken and the arresting action provided by an hydraulic system below decks, complete details of which are withheld. Even should a pilot give his engine 'full gun' after having caught the wire he is still held back tenaciously.

While at sea in Courageous we were able (due to fog and suspension of flying) to cross over to HMS *Scimitar*, the attendant 'safety' S-Class destroyer which sticks doggedly astern on the port side. Her commander told us something of how his ship co-operates with the *Courageous*. When the carrier hoists the 'aeroplane flag' at the dip, hands are piped to their 'flying stations'. Before flying starts the crash party mans the rescue boat which hangs ready at its davits, equipped with fire extinguishers, grapnel, axe, cutters and lifebouys and first-aid equipment. A second party is detailed to man the rescue derrick installed on the forecastle. This party is provided with a boat-hook and grapnel, heaving lines and a lifebuoy attached to a heaving line. In the event of a crash the First Lieutenant would pass word to the rescue boat by megaphone.

Sitting in a boat for hours on end in the North Sea on a winter's day can distinctly unpleasant, despite oil-skins, but the crew of the *Scimitar*'s crash boat seemed not only cheery but interested in the operations of the great grey carrier off their starboard bow.

We left *Courageous* with one regret: that we had seen none of the new Blackburn Skua fleet fighter dive bomber monoplanes. Actually a flight of Skuas had landed on the day before our arrival but had left again for Donibristle. One heard some highly enthusiastic reports, auguring well for the success of these and other advanced types, which will see service with our Naval Air Branch.

Chapter 4

Bloody Fools or Bloody Heroes!

TAG Les Sayer describes his part in the first attack on the *Bismarck* on May 24, 1941.

One minute, I was in a newly formed squadron, with new pilots, doing dummy deck landings, and the next minute, embarking on the carrier HMS *Victorious*, which had a hangar full of Spitfires all in packing cases. I wondered what it was all about, and only began to get a vague idea when special authority was given to all TAGs to buy one pound of chocolate from the NAAFI. In those days, there were no such things as survival kits, and it seemed to me that there was a distinct possibility of finishing up in Greenland, with a comforting pound of chocolate to keep out the cold. That we were obliged to buy it ourselves out of our own very meagre pay seems incredible today, but it was something we took quite for granted at that time.

Then came the long period of waiting for something to happen. Half way up to the bridge of the carrier, reached by narrow ladders, there was a small 'caboose' and there the TAGs waited. Six of

Iconic image of 825 Squadron on the stern of HMS *Victorious*, ranged for take-off on May 24, 1941. (*Aeroplane*)

them, in flying kit, wedged themselves into this uncomfortable space, which rapidly filled with smoke and an aroma your best friends wouldn't tell you about. Apprehensive eyes, not quite knowing where to look, focused on good luck charms tied to their Mae Wests.

There were periods of uneasy silence broken only by the steady drone of the ventilation system and the occasional clang of the sliding door, when someone went out to nowhere in particular and came back from the same place.

The boredom ends

It seemed only yesterday that these people, now labelled TAGs, were happily cleaning windows, reading gas meters, mixing medicines or waiting for the next grouse shoot. Now, here they were, about to embark into the unknown, uttering newly acquired nautical phrases, which under the circumstances were almost meaningless except in so far as

THE *BISMARCK*	
BUILDER	Blohm & Voss, Hamburg
COMMISSIONED	Aug 24, 1940
DISPLACEMENT	41,700 tons (standard)
	50,300 tons (loaded)
LENGTH	823ft (overall)
BEAM	118ft
DRAFT	31ft
SPEED	30kts
RANGE	8,870 miles at 19kts
COMPLEMENT	103 officers, 1,962 enlisted men
ARMAMENT	8 x 15in, 12 x 5.9in, 16 x 4.1in,
	16 x 1.5in & 12 x 0.79in

The *Bismarck* pictured from the *Prinz Eugen* making for the Atlantic only a few weeks before it was sunk by the combined efforts of a few Swordfish and the Royal Navy. (via Owen Cooper)

An epic tale which was big news during the war; the successful action led to the book by Frank Brannand, which was followed by the equally successful film in 1960, *Sink the Bismarck*, starring Kenneth Moore.

they illustrated the nervous tension caused by what they knew was to come.

Suddenly the boredom of the long wait ended. Leaving the briefing room, someone cut a pack of cards on his way out and turned up the three of spades. 'Ah, well,' he commented, 'it could have been the ace!'

The *Victorious* was going flat out as the TAGs emerged onto the wet, pitching flight deck and walked toward the rather pathetic looking range of Swordfish, plodding, first uphill then down, along the heaving deck.

Each Swordfish was armed with a live torpedo and on the warheads of many had been scrawled rude messages, many of which were being rapidly washed off by the intermittent avalanches of heavy spray churned up by the ship's speedy pursuit of the *Bismarck* in rather unkind weather.

Getting airborne was no problem, there was plenty of wind to give us lift off the deck. Soon, in loose formation, a gaggle of antiquated biplanes was on a two-hour journey to attack the mightiest ship afloat.

825 SQUADRON ORDER OF BATTLE AND MAY 24, 1941

1st Sub-Flight

(5)A+	Lt Cdr E K Esmonde, Lt C C Ennever & PO S E Parker
(5)C	Sub Lt J C Thompson, Lt R L Parkinson & PO A L Johnson
(5)B	Lt N G MacLean, Sub Lt L Bailey & PO D A Bunce

2nd Sub-Flight

(5)F+	Lt P D Gick, Sub Lt V K Norfolk & PO L D Sayer
(5)G	Lt W F C Garthwaite, Sub Lt W A Gillingham & LA H T A Wheeler
(5)H/V4337	Sub Lt P B Jackson, Sub Lt D A Berrill & LA F. G. Sparkes

3rd Sub-Flight

(5)K	Lt H C M Pollard, Sub Lt D M Beattie & LA P W Clitheroe, DSM
(5)L	Sub Lt R G Lawson, Sub Lt F L Robinson & LA I L Owen
(5)M	Sub Lt A J Houston, Sub Lt J R Geater & PO W J Clinton

HOW THE GERMANS DESCRIBED THE ATTACK ON MAY 24, 1941

"They came in flying low over the water, launched their torpedoes and zoomed away. Flak was pouring from every gun barrel but didn't seem to hit them. The first torpedo hissed past 150yds in front of the *Bismarck*'s bow. The second did the same and the third. Helmsman Hansen was operating the press buttons of the steering gear as, time and time again, the *Bismarck* manoeuvred out of danger. She evaded a fifth and then a sixth, when yet another torpedo darted straight towards the ship. A few seconds later a tremendous shudder ran through the hull and a towering column of water rose at *Bismarck*'s side. The nickel-chrome-steel armour plate of her ship's side survived the attack..."

An 810 Squadron Swordfish takes off from HMS *Ark Royal* on May 26, 1941. It was its squadrons that damaged *Bismarck* sufficiently enough for the battleship to finally fall to the guns of the Royal Navy.

HMS *Victorious* had only been commissioned for two weeks when it became embroiled in the hunt for the *Bismarck* along with the HMS *King George V, Repulse* and four cruisers from Force H out of Gibraltar. (Via Owen Cooper)

In the starboard firing step I had secreted a strictly illegal tot of rum, to bring an inner warmth and a degree of comfort to the stark realisation that here, over the North Atlantic, hundreds of miles from anything that could be called remotely friendly, were a handful of blokes doing what they had been trained to do.

Nestling a little more comfortably in my Sidcot flying suit, I wiggled my toes in my flying boots, checked the rear gun, hoped I was tuned into the right spot on the dial on the radio, and gazed through a small hole where I could see the red fin of the live torpedo slung underneath. I fervently hoped that I would soon see that disappear on its way to its mark.

I had great faith in my pilot, a Dartmouth type, with great determination laced with an ability to assess critical situations and make the right decisions. Anyway, seated in the rear cockpit, there was nothing I could do about it.

Then, quite suddenly, there was this monster, steaming at high speed with all guns blazing and looking like the dying embers of a wood fire caught in a draught. Then a muffled voice down the voice pipe, which announced in matter of fact tones, "Going in."

During the long, straight run necessary for the pilot to get his sights lined up, I stood up and unseated the rear gun, with the intention of getting off a few rounds if the opportunity arose. Closer and closer we came, anticipating the upward surge of the aircraft as she was relieved of the weight of the torpedo. A violent turn away from *Bismarck*, and frenzied evasive action threw me back in my seat, from whence, to my horror, I saw the fin of the torpedo still in place.

As confused thoughts tumbled through my mind, there came that same calm, muffled voice, "I'm going around again. Not quite lined up."

After coming all this way and getting near enough to spit at *Bismarck*, we were going around again? This was no practice run. Those pretty fireflies racing toward us were tracer bullets and what they hit they hurt.

How can we miss?

As we left *Bismarck*'s immediate vicinity, to begin our turn for a second run in, I had an uninterrupted view of the ship still going flat out, and watched the other aircraft climbing away as they turned for home. Now we were quite alone and going round again. At about 25 miles out and still at wave top height, we turned to face our target for the second time. This time, we had the dubious honour of having *Bismarck*'s undivided attention. With her whole massive armament free to concentrate on one frail, canvas covered, obsolete biplane, how could they fail to destroy us? One torpedo, two light machine guns and three men against the might of the German Navy and what a hope!

Standing up, I looked over the pilot's shoulder, everything was uncannily quiet, we had not yet been spotted, or perhaps they could not believe what they had spotted. Closer and closer, the battleship got bigger and bigger, and now my thoughts changed to wondering, 'How can we miss?' The target was huge and the run-in perfect.

The upward surge, as the torpedo was dropped and the elation of an almost certain hit was wiped out by the desperate need to get away from *Bismarck*'s entire armament. We had proved, almost literally, a pain in their rear, and they definitely resented it! The hurled everything at us, including their main armament of 11in guns, which had so recently blown up our most powerful battleship and sorely damaged another. They were trying to knock our still low flying aircraft out of the sky, with the splashes from shells of these formidable guns. To avoid the fate intended for us, we had to watch the flashes of these guns and count the seconds before the shells threw up the almighty splashes, making sure that we weren't where they were!

A close run thing

One such splash was near enough to tear the fabric from beneath my seat, and permitted a howling gale to blow through the resultant hole. Thereafter, I complained to the pilot, "It's bloody draughty back here!"

Clear at last, we set course for where we hoped our ship would be, the immense relief being somewhat marred by wondering if we had enough fuel to reach her. This was a time when there were few aids to navigation, and for one moving pinpoint to rendezvous with another in the vastness of the Atlantic was, in itself, no mean feat, the more so after the let-down inevitably felt by men who had passed through, to put it mildly, a frightening experience.

Mercifully, the *Victorious* broke all regulations and switched on her light beacon, the rest was easy. All the aircraft made it, but with very little fuel to spare.

Going below, there were those same faces that saw us off some hours before, plainly thinking, 'bloody fool', or 'bloody hero', according to temperament. Eggs and bacon and a tot of rum and it was all over.

Chapter 5

Against All Odds

The passage of the German capital ships *Scharnhorst*, *Gneisenau* and *Prinz Eugen* through the English Channel has been recorded many times over the years. What follows is an account by TAG Don Bunce, one of the five survivors of the ill-fated attack.

Taking part in a 'fiasco'

Making our way to the dispersal, on that February day, the weather was no different to the previous days, bitterly cold, with snow covering the grass airfield. Blissfully unaware that we were taking part in a 'fiasco', what dominated our minds was that a planned night attack was now to take place at midday. As usual, TAGs were excluded from the briefing sessions and had to rely on the Observer for any 'Gen'. Four TAGs (including myself), one former pilot of mine, one Observer, and, of course, Esmonde himself, had taken part in the torpedo attack on the *Bismarck*, from HMS *Victorious*, and we were only

too aware of the implications of a daylight action. This time it was not the middle of the North Atlantic, but the Straits of Dover, and a warning was ringing in our ears from the RAF types in the mess: a new German fighter, the Fw190, was now operational.

We took off and formed up over the coast, and I well remember exchanging a 'thumbs up' sign with fellow TAG 'Ginger' Johnson, just before seeing Spitfires overhead, and assumed all our escort had arrived; we were already at sea level. Soon after, we were headed out to sea, in line ahead formation. I was in the first flight of three, with Esmonde leading, our aircraft bringing up the rear. The second flight was some distance from us, still in 'V' formation, and I cannot recall seeing them again. I began to prepare the VGO machine gun, loading a magazine and then sitting down and waiting. The weather was overcast, with low cloud and poor visibility, and the Spitfires were just below the cloud base. Perhaps at this point, I should remind the reader, and indeed myself, just how short actions of this sort are; everything happens so quickly. Trying to recall it now gives a type of 'time lapse' element to the story.

Fw190 target practice

At this stage, with the Spitfires weaving overhead in an attempt to stay with us, I ventured a look forward and, through the mist, saw a destroyer. Then it all happened: tracer from the destroyer 'floated' our way, that is, until it came close, when it took on the characteristics of an express train, and in came

The battleship *Scharnhorst*, one of the primary targets for Operation *Fuller* on February 12, 1941 and for the Germans, Operation *Cerberus* to bring fleet back to Germany.

the Fw190s. I have no recollection of how many there were, but only concentrated on those that were on our tail. It seemed endless; as soon as one peeled off another was in its place, with tracer speeding toward us.

What was my reaction? Apart from using every Naval swear word I could muster, my instinct appeared to be to place as much of the feeble .303in tracer in front of the 190s as I could, stoppages permitting; all drill in this respect went overboard, as indeed went any malfunctioning

Left: Lt Cdr Eugene Kingsmill Esmonde VC, DSO, the commanding officer of 825 Squadron from May 13, 1940 to November 13, 1941 and again from January 1, 1942 to his demise on February 12, 1942.

Below: The only ship in the same class as the *Scharnhorst* was the *Gneisenau* which was commissioned on May 21, 1938. While the battleship managed to escape to Kiel as part of Operation *Cerberus*, *Gneisenau* played no further part in the Second World War.

magazine. There simply isn't time to do other than that. The whole affair, from my backward viewpoint, was developing into a practice shoot for Fw190s, and we were the drogue target; they were coming so close. As they peeled off to the port I had a sideways clear view of the pilot. I had a quick visual image of the shells hitting the water, giving them perfect alignment to hit the old Swordfish.

Strange to say, throughout the entire action, I had no impending sense of danger or injury to myself, despite all the hardware being thrown at us. I just considered myself 'fireproof'. Alas, my Pilot and Observer were less fortunate, both being hit.

Just as suddenly as it had started, the fighters left. Presumably our torpedo had been launched; one is usually aware of the drop, but not on this occasion. Now I could look around. I turned, to sit down, and found a gaping hole to the port side of the seat. Gingerly, I tried sitting, in order to send some kind of distress signal, but the wireless set was dead. However, the IFF worked, and I immediately switched to the distress position, but as this relied on radar contact, at sea level, this must have been a useless exercise.

Taking casualties

At about this time, I turned to the Observer, 'Mac' Samples, (although I didn't refer to him as 'Mac' in those days, but over the years we have become firm friends) to ask if he was ok. In reply, he reached down with one hand and brought it up covered in blood; his leg and foot were badly injured. It appeared the Pilot, Pat Kingsmill, was also hurt in the lower leg at the same time.

A glance to starboard showed a group of small boats and MTBs? And we appeared to be heading for them. As we closed, their true identity was revealed: they were E-Boats, and gunfire from them immediately began hitting us, and Pat, with great skill, began to crab away, and I, with further oaths, emptied my last magazine in their direction.

Above: One of only five survivors from the Swordfish attack, Sub Lt Edgar Frederick Lee (left) chats with Wg Cdr Tom Gleave outside the Officers' Mess at Manston on February 13, 1942.

Left: Glad to be alive, Don Bunce's pilot (left), Sub Lt Charles Major 'Pat' Kingsmill and his observer, Sub Lt Reginald McCartney Samples recovering from their injuries in March 1942.

OPERATION *FULLER* SWORDFISH CREWS

1 Sub-Flight

'H'/W5984   Lt Cdr E Esmonde DSO, Lt W H Williams & PO W J Clinton

'L'/W5907   Sub Lt C M Kingsmill*, Sub Lt R McC Samples* & LA D A Bunce*

'G'/W5983   Sub Lt B W Rose*, Sub Lt E F Lee* & PO A L Johnson DSM

2 Sub-Flight

'F'/V4523   Lt J C Thompson, Sub Lt E H F Wright, & LA E Tapping

'K'/W5985   Sub Lt C R Wood, Sub Lt R L Parkinson & LA T A Wheeler

'L'/W5978   Sub Lt P Bligh, Sub Lt W Beynon & LA W G Smith

It was all the old Swordfish could do to crab, because the damage was considerable, and we began to assume a tail-down position. Then, suddenly, great flashes streaked down the port side; a large square hole in the upper main plane meant that the dinghy had been shot away; the marine distress flare was lodged in place, and our last encounter with the E-Boats must have ignited it; a few more flashes and it sputtered out. What of the rest of the damage? The Stringbag was beginning to live up to its nickname. Everywhere a shell had passed through the fabric, a three-cornered tear had appeared; there was no fabric at all on the port tail plane. Oil was dripping down the starboard fuselage, where the oil cooler had been punctured. Pat Kingsmill told me afterwards that it is quite normal to be able to see three cylinders of the Pegasus engine. Two were shot away, and we still managed to fly; not for long though: with the tail well down, we ditched perfectly.

Photographs of 825 Squadron during the period of Operation *Fuller* are incredibly rare and this image is of one of the replacement aircraft operating from Lee-on-Solent following the unit's reformation.

ML rescue

Mac and I could see a single MTB type boat on the starboard and, as we appeared to be heading that way, I was convinced that Pat had seen it too, but, no, it was a pure coincidence, we dropped into the sea a few hundred yards short. It was a Motor Minelayer (ML), sent out for just this purpose. On impact, I hit my harness release button and threw it off, then, literally, stepped overboard into the Channel, to help Mac. A jerk on my head told me that I had forgotten to unplug the headphones and, quickly yanking off my helmet, I found that Mac had floated free. The ML was now alongside, and I hung back, thinking that I might be able to help the others, but was 'politely' informed that, if I was ok, to get out and leave it to the experts. I was grateful, for it was extremely cold! Once aboard, I was bundled down below, to lie between the giant diesel engines, given dry clothes and a cup of 'pussers' rum. Pat Kingsmill was in the wheelhouse, and Mac Samples lay on the after deck, a big matelot attempting to keep him warm, for his injuries were quite severe. The passage to Ramsgate harbour, at full speed through a choppy sea, must have been a nightmare to the other two. The rum helped me, but the roar of the engines precluded any conversation, leaving me with my own thoughts.

An ambulance was waiting on the quayside and quickly whipped us off to hospital. The others received treatment immediately, and I was left to loaf about the corridor until transport picked me up that evening. I did manage a bedside visit before leaving, but it was to be many years before I was to see them again.

No news is not good news

I now began to look forward, with some trepidation, for news of my mates. Edgar Lee, (Observer in the second aircraft) who, too, was uninjured, must have arrived back at Manston at about the same time as I did, his pilot, Rose, told me. Rose had severe back injuries but, to my dismay, his TAG, 'Ginger' Johnson DSM, had been killed early in the action. There was no news of the rest, but there was still hope. Next morning, it became increasingly evident we who had made it back were to be the only ones!

The impact of this must have put me in a kind of daze, and it didn't help when, along with the PO Fitter, we were ordered to assemble and pack the kit of the other five TAGs. Stowing photographs and other personal items was very traumatic, but it had to be done, and rather me than anyone else. Quite how I arrived back at Lee-on-Solent escapes me. I vaguely remember being hauled out in front of Sunday Divisions, with Edgar Lee, to be told that we were some kind of heroes. A week or so later, the *Daily Mirror* front page announced, along with the VC for Esmonde, DSOs for the officers; the CGM had come my way. What was the CGM? Nobody could tell me! The rest of the squadron were 'Mentioned in Dispatches'.

'Buy' your own ribbon

During this time, I saw no Medical Officer, nor indeed anyone else, except when passing 'Jimmy the One' (The First Lieutenant, also referred to as 'Number One'; second in command on a ship). One morning, he stopped me and asked why I wasn't wearing my medal ribbon. 'No idea what it looks like, Sir,' I replied.

With that, he hauled me off to examine the records, and eventually came up with the 'gen'. It was some time before I could trace a source and 'buy' some.

Counselling, of course, wasn't heard of in those days, so I was packed off on leave, with the idea, no doubt, that it was a cure for everything! It was, perhaps, the worst thing that could happen. All my mates from pre-service days were either in the Services themselves, or working all hours, so I became completely isolated.

> **THE VOICE OF THE ENEMY**
>
> 'What an heroic stage for them to meet their end! Behind them their homeland, which they had just left with their hearts steeled to their purpose, still in view'.

At one point, I became so disturbed that I was afraid to cross the road and, in those, days, even in the centre of Oxford, you couldn't say there was a traffic problem. What of my fellow TAGs whose experiences that day easily overshadowed my own? Some of us had been together for almost twelve months; it seemed much longer.

Remembering the TAGs

Jack, or 'Clints', Clinton had been in the third sub-flight on the *Bismarck* attack, and on that day was TAG to Esmonde. At the height of the action, he was seen outside the cockpit, astride the fuselage, beating out a fire with his hands, witnessed by a Spitfire pilot. I'm sure that if this had been known at the time he would have collected a VC, like his pilot. His swap of duties with Les Sayer, our Squadron PO, is well known, and must give Les the miss of the century. 'Clints' is buried at St James Church, Ruislip. Laurence 'Ginger' Johnson and I were alongside each other in the first sub-flight on the Bismarck attack, and retained the same position that day. He was awarded the DSM, after the *Bismarck* action. My abiding memory of 'Ginger' is on the *Ark Royal.* Every time he was flying, you could always see his father, a member of the Ship's Company, waiting anxiously for his return. I received a very sad letter, many years later, from 'Pop' Johnson. No doubt, by now, he has joined his son on that Final Draft.

Henry Wheeler had been in the second sub-flight against the *Bismarck* and is best known for the yarns he could spin on being a gasman in London.

Ernest 'Horse' Tapping joined us, I think, on the *Ark Royal,* and was famed for his consumption of beer. The rest of us tried to keep in step at those very enjoyable lunch-time sessions in the NAAFI at Lee, prior to moving down to Manston.

William 'Bill' Smith had joined us, again, on the 'Ark'. His family were Thames watermen, a career he intended to follow. Smithy is at rest a few yards from Lt Cdr Esmonde, in Gillingham cemetery. Nothing is known of the fate of the second sub-flight that day. They were led by my pilot on the *Bismarck* action, Lt Thompson, and also included my pilot from the *Ark Royal,* Sub Lt Wood, an ex-Rating Pilot.

Chapter 6

Running Straight and True

Nothing to it!

The Air Crew Torpedo Manual, AP.2459A, states that 'Dropping a torpedo from aircraft is a highly skilled job.' It certainly was, and only time and constant practice improved the proficiency of the crew delivering such a weapon. One of their difficulties was that no matter how often you trained, nothing could simulate the conditions during an actual attack under fire and in bad weather. The Manual further states that,

'To get the best out of the torpedo, one of the first things you have to do in dropping it from an aircraft is to give it a 'good entry' into the water. After that, providing you have sighted correctly and set a proper depth setting, the torpedo should do the rest.'

Simple, isn't it! It was this 'good entry' that had been the subject of much research, including what happens during the torpedo's flight through the air – the period between releasing it from the aircraft and its entry into water. In the 'good old days' torpedoes were dropped at very low heights and very

While an airmen scurries to his Swordfish another is loaded with an 18in torpedo during exercises by the TTU at Gosport in the spring of 1939. (*Aeroplane*)

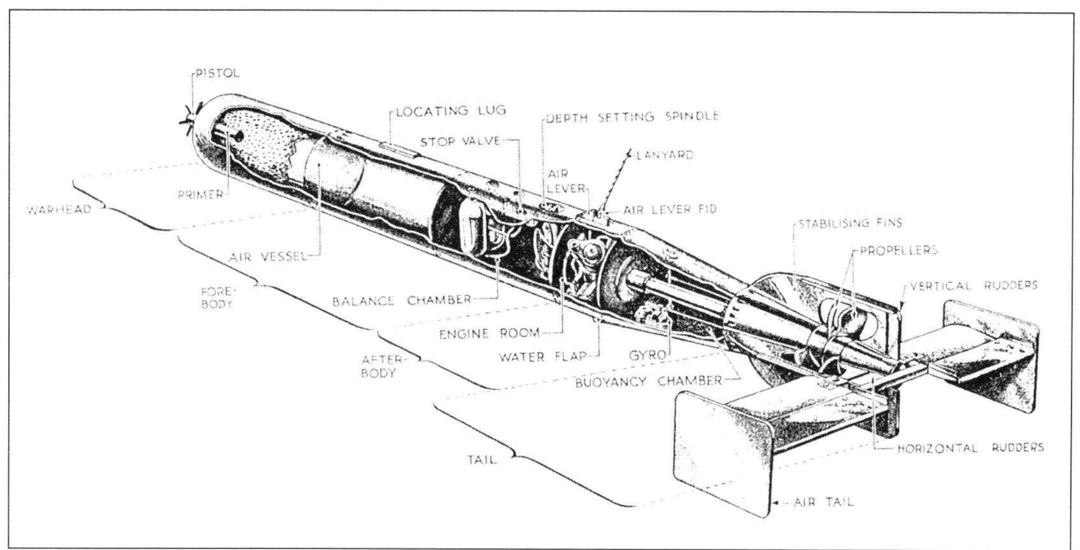

The inner workings of a standard 18in Mk IX Torpedo which dated back to the post-First World War period but was still in service when the Swordfish arrived and as such was carried during the type's early career.

slow speeds so that the time of flight in air was short and any external forces acting on the torpedo negligible. This did mean, however, that the torpedo could only be dropped from certain types of slow aircraft and that the type of attack was very limited.

The Torpedo in the Air

As aircraft developed, the speed and height of dropping also increased, and this started to have an effect on the flight of the torpedo through the air. Generally speaking, an 18in torpedo had to be dropped so that the trajectory angle was between 14° and 24°, the trajectory being the actual path of the centre of gravity of the torpedo in the air after its release. An angle below 14° usually resulted in a bellyflop, while above 24° degrees the torpedo would enter a steep dive. Another way to achieve a bellyflop was to drop too fast and too low, giving a very low trajectory angle.

No fixed dropping height and speed were laid down, these depending on the type of aircraft. The parameters for delivery by the Swordfish and Albacore were known and practised constantly at torpedo training units and later on operational squadrons. As an example, at a dropping height of 100ft (30m) and a speed of 120kt (220km/h), the time of flight in the air would be 2.5 seconds, covering 170yd (155m). But let John Kilbracken take you through:

'Dropping a torpedo is an extremely tricky business. It weighs getting on for a ton and should be dropped into the sea from a height of 50-70ft. After entering the water, it runs on its own power at 25kt a few feet below the surface for over 2,000yd unless anything gets in its way, in which case it goes off bang with devastating effect. A single torpedo (also known as a tin-fish) can sink a merchantman. The trickiness lies in the fact that you have to be flying at the correct low speed, and as straight and level as possible, and at the right altitude, at the moment you release it and for several subsequent seconds, if it's going to run accurately or indeed run at all. This is none too simple if your target is the friendly Brigadier, our usual target vessel in the Firth of Forth. It's quite a different matter if the tracer is coming at you from a heavily defended enemy fleet or convoy. Another little matter is that over a minute will elapse, if you drop from 1,000yd, before the tin-fish reaches its target, which will meantime have travelled 800yd if steaming at 20kt. You must judge her speed, aim the right distance ahead and guess

The pilot of Swordfish I L7652 '2' of the TTU demonstrates how to drop a torpedo at the correct angle during an official display for senior military staff in 1930. (*Aeroplane*)

what avoiding action she may take. Our attacks would start from several thousand feet, whence we would dive seaward, spend not more than ten seconds at sea level if possible, then climb steeply away for home. Our first efforts were made light, then we'd fly with a dummy torpedo weighing 1,600lb. In both cases a camera automatically took a picture at the moment you pressed the tit (button), from which could be computed your altitude, attitude, range and, given the speed of the target vessel, whether you would have hit her. Later, we dropped 'runners', which were the same as real torpedoes but without the explosive charge, set to run deep so that they would pass under the target vessel and then rise to the surface for recovery. Otherwise the tin-fish, worth several thousand pounds, would he badly damaged on impact and very probably lost. They were so scarce and valuable that we were rationed to three drops each! In 23 attacks I scored nineteen hits and all four misses were less than 30yd.'

The art of 'guesstimation'

Assuming the vertical aspects are ignored at this stage the aiming and delivery of the torpedo is exactly like trying to hit a rabbit on the run; that is, you have to lay off for the distance the rabbit will have covered by the time your missile gets there. It all stems back to the triangle of velocities, but in this case it had to be reproduced and solved to give an aim-off angle before the torpedo was actually dropped. Basically, the three factors are the target's speed, angle on the bow and the average torpedo speed. The target's speed had to be 'guesstimated', especially under combat conditions, although the speeds of enemy ships were usually known; the angle on the bow was set ideally at 60°; and the average torpedo speed was 27kt or 40kt. All the pilot had to do was to put his head against the rest provided to eliminate parallax error, sight his lamps and press the plunger to release the torpedo. The sight fitted to Swordfish and Albacore aircraft was known as a bar torpedo sight and consisted of a row of lamps mounted on a bar outside the cockpit in front of the windscreen. The lamps were spaced so that the angle subtended at the pilot's eye by two successive lamps was 4°, so they represented 4° steps. The lamps were operated by a selector switch calibrated in knots to represent a ship's speed.

As mentioned previously, once it leaves the aircraft the torpedo is unstable: unless it is controlled in some way it may oscillate about its trajectory and could enter the water in any attitude, or even somersault. Ideally the torpedo should enter the water with its nose approximately along the correct trajectory. Like a dart, which has feathers to stabilize its flight, the most obvious way to stabilize the flight of a torpedo was to add an air tail. Early trials made with simple fixed tails were not very successful, but later they had an air tail control gear. This was mounted on or inside the torpedo and moved the tail in such a way it damped out any oscillation in the trajectory once dropped. Once the torpedo entered the water the air tail would break away so that it would not interfere with the run. Once again, all is not simple. Theoretically, the air tail should be of a size that allowed control of the torpedo under any dropping conditions. However, the layout of many torpedo-carrying aircraft was unsuitable for the fitting of a large air tail, so different tails would be required for each type of aircraft carrying them. Also, the slipstream of the aircraft influenced the airflow around the tail and upset any control.

To overcome these problems a device known as a drum control gear was fitted, which served two purposes. The first was to keep the torpedo steady until it was clear of the aircraft's slipstream and the second was to help the air tail by inclining the nose of the torpedo at the right trajectory when released. The drum control gear consisted of two pulleys fixed to a shaft, which in turn was attached to a flywheel that could be loaded with weights. Two wires of equal length were wound round each of the two pulleys, with the end of each wire attached to the tail of the torpedo. Once the torpedo was released the pull on the wires caused the flywheel and pulleys to revolve; the inertia of the flywheel opposed this and in doing so caused tension in the wires, which pulled up on the tail. As an example,

An 18in Mk XII torpedo, most likely a practice round, being loaded aboard a Swordfish in this pre-war scene. The torpedo was carried on a pair of crutches and secured by a wire which connected to a quick-release mechanism. (*Aeroplane*)

DUNLOP

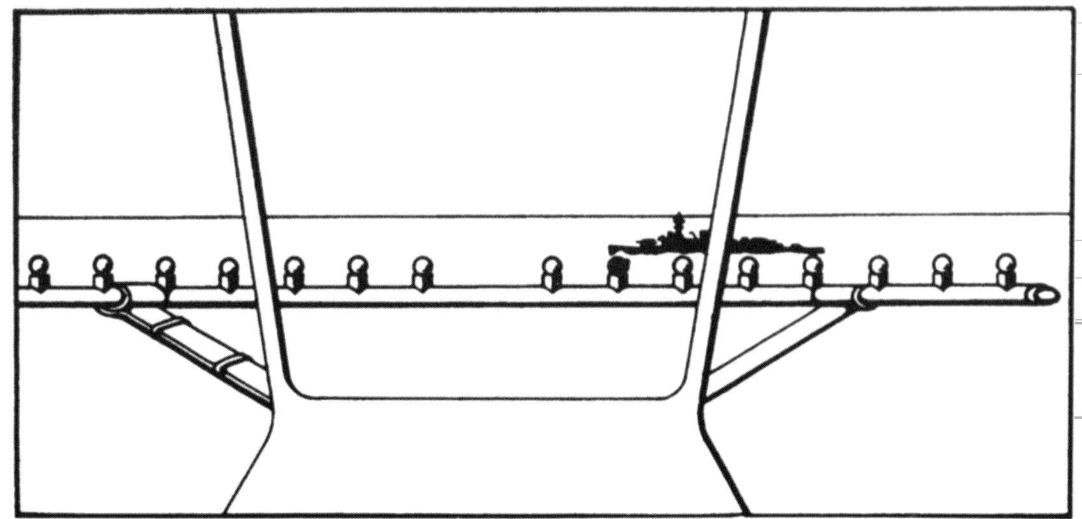

The simple, yet effective 'bar sight' used by the pilot of a Swordfish to indicate when to release his torpedo. In this example the black light is the point at which the torpedo would have been released. (W. A. Harrison)

if the torpedo rolled to the left the right wire became slack and the pull on the drum control system was thrown on the left side, correcting the roll. Simultaneously the wires pulled the nose of the torpedo down, imparting an angular velocity that hopefully set up the correct trajectory. During the first few seconds after release the torpedo was still attached to the aircraft by these wires and the pilot had to fly straight and level until it was clear. This is aptly described by Lt Cdr E. W. Whitley:

'I was an Air Fitter and Leading Air Fitter in 819 Squadron in Illustrious during 1940-41 when one of my jobs was to wind the 21½ feet of cable on the two spools of the Drum Control Gear, located just behind the TAG's cockpit. These were attached to the air tail of the 'fish', and as they wound off the weighted shaft the tail was delayed to get the right drop angle. I did all the ones for the Taranto raid. The ship ran out of rubber bands that held the wire on the spools and I was sent ashore at Alexandria to buy some. I got lost and at 18 years of age found myself without a single white face or a policeman in sight! I was getting a bit worried until one of the ladies, only eyes being visible, said "Good Morning!"'

The main reason for having the drum control gear was that the air tail operated on a horizontal axis, and although it had vertical stabilizers, any slight deviation in roll and/or yaw would result in the torpedo running erratically once in the water. In fact, if there was considerable roll, the horizontal action of the air tail then acted as a rudder again, resulting in erratic running, in this case, vertically up or down! Therefore a considerable amount of piloting skill was required to deliver a torpedo accurately, and only constant practice would provide those skills. The aircraft had to be flown into the attacking position with much verve and held there until the right distance for release was reached, followed by the wait for those vital couple of seconds after the torpedo had been released before being able to pull away.

The Torpedo in the Water

Once the torpedo entered the water it plunged to its best operating depth for the attack, an average plunge for a good delivery being around 40ft (12m). On the initial plunge, as it descended below its set depth to run, the depth gear inside the torpedo activated and turned the horizontal rudders in the torpedo tail upwards, ending its dive and gradually stabilizing its path. The initial dive, known as the plunge, took up about 30yd (27m) of the torpedo's run in the water, during which it decelerated from its airspeed to its set water speed.

Other factors had to be taken into consideration for the torpedo attack to be successful. These were the Recovery Range, the Arming or Safety Range, and the Minimum and Maximum Running Range. The Recovery Range is the distance the torpedo travelled in water, measured from the point of entry to the point that it commenced its run at the correct depth; that is, after all the variables dampen down so that it runs at its pre-determined depth, usually after around 250-300yd (230-270m). The Arming Range is the distance in water the torpedo runs to arm the firing pistol, and that depended on the type of pistol fitted. If the length of flight in the air is added to the Arming Range, this is the Minimum Dropping Range, the minimum distance from the target that the torpedo could be dropped so that the pistol was armed when it reached its target. The Maximum Running Range was from the point of entry to where the torpedo crossed the target's track and then, if no hit was made, the distance the torpedo travelled before running out of steam and sinking. If the torpedo was set to run at 40kt, the Maximum Running Range was in the region of 2,000yd (1,800m). If set to run at 27kt the Maximum Running Range was 3,000-4,000yd (2,700-3,700m).

The aim of the torpedo attack was to strike the enemy ship at a depth where it would do most damage. Naval ships would have some protection below the waterline such as armour, bulges and side compartments, which, if hit, would hopefully only flood, rather than cause the ship to sink. Other factors were the shape of the hull and draught depth when loaded and empty: too shallow a setting might mean the torpedo running below the keel.

THE 18IN MK XII TORPEDO AND TECHNICAL INFORMATION

SERVICE	FAA & RAF Coastal Command from 1937-1945
WEIGHT	1,548lb
LENGTH	16ft 3in
DIAMETER	17.72in
WARHEAD	388lb of TNT
SPEED	40kts for 1,500yds 47kts for 3,500yds

A fine display of torpedoes, complete with their trolleys and hydraulic jacks which made light work of raising the weapon up to the crutches on the underside of the fuselage. This is Crail and the Albacores in the background belong to 785 and 786 Squadrons. (via R. C. Sturtivant)

Excellent public relations photograph, taken January 23, 1941, showing ratings being trained in the art of loading a torpedo onto, in this case, an Albacore that has already been relegated to the second line while the Swordfish remained firmly in place. (Central Press Photos via *Aeroplane*)

A Jackdaw on My Sleeve: RNAS Crail and the Swordfish Years

The Swordfish in Fife

On November 4, 1940, the first of two dedicated squadrons were formed as TBR training squadrons. 785 Squadron, under the command of Lt Cdr P G O Sydney-Turner, was the first training unit to be formed at Crail. Initially equipped with 13 Blackburn Sharks and five Swordfish, within a few months

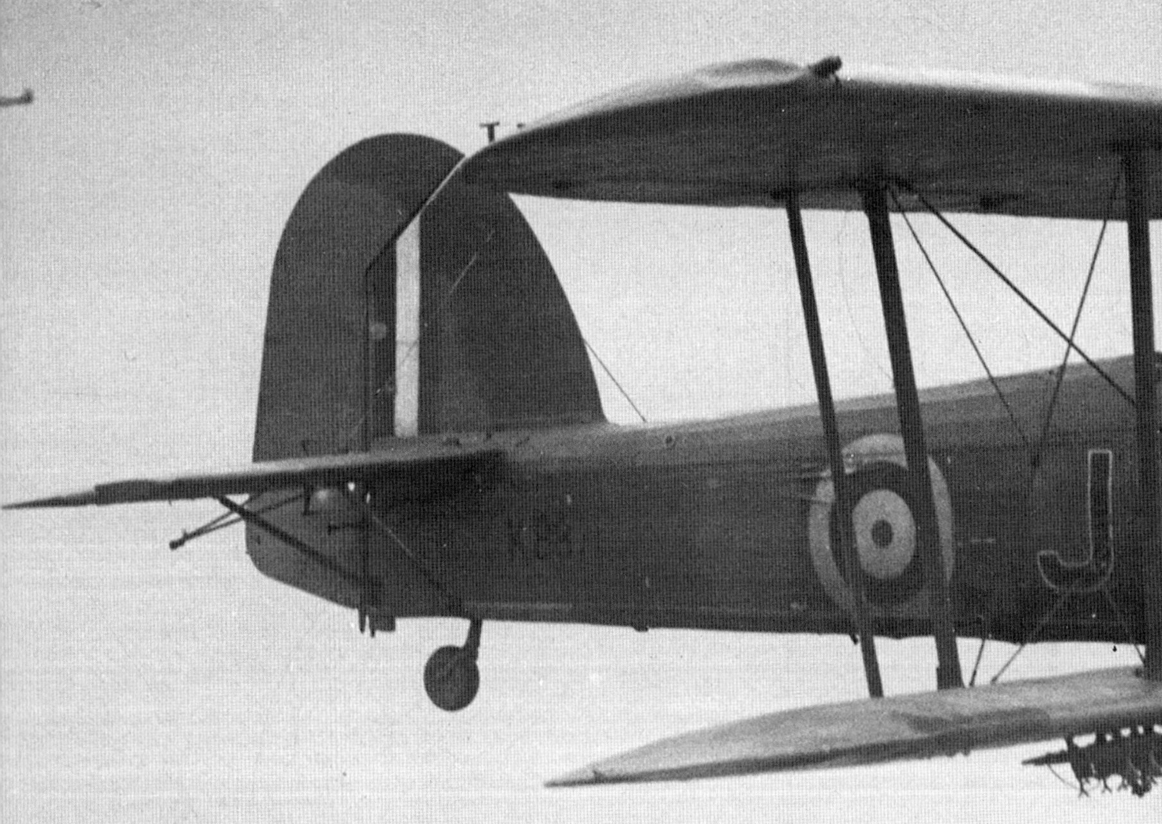

Originally delivered to the TTU at Gosport in April 1937, Swordfish I, K8871 'J' was one of the first aircraft to arrive at Crail on November 7, 1940 for service with 785/786 Squadrons. It was also one of the first to depart; it was wrecked in an accident on July 16, 1941. (via Martyn Chorlton)

Sharks were deemed obsolete for TBR training. In August 1941 the Shark was replaced by the Albacore, which in turn was introduced to replace the Swordfish in FAA service. However, the superb Swordfish, affectionately known as the 'Stringbag' would continue to serve the FAA throughout the Second World War and would score more successes against the enemy than the Albacore ever achieved.

786 Squadron was the second TBR training squadron to be formed at Crail on November 21, 1940. Under the command of Capt F W Brown, the unit was first equipped with nine Albacores and was specifically formed to operate alongside 785 Squadron. 786 Squadron increased in size from mid-1941 when it began to receive the Swordfish and the rare American-built Vought-Sikorsky Chesapeake I.

TBR Training

All pilots throughout the Second World War who passed through Crail would have been specifically selected for TBR training at an early stage in their military flying careers. Initially, they were taught to fly at very low levels over the sea whilst carrying a dummy torpedo. Although this sounds quite straightforward, travelling at high speed at 200ft above the waves took a great deal of concentration and many crews were lost in the process. The next stage was practice attacks on the many target ships which were at Crail's disposal, anchored, or moving in the Firth of Forth. The vast majority of these ships were

A pair of Swordfish Is of 785 Squadron at Crail being loaded with 18in training torpedoes.

retired paddle steamers, cross channel ferries and several obsolete Royal Navy ships. All were too large to berth at Crail village so they operated from Methil docks on the edge of Largo Bay.

Once the trainee crews were proficient at approaching the target ship safely, they graduated to actually dropping a dummy torpedo. The dummies were in short supply during the early years of the war and the next stage of dropping a 'runner' was reached as quickly as possible. A 'runner' was exactly the same as the real thing but without a warhead. They were also set to run deeper than a live example and once they had run their course, the torpedo would rise to the surface for recovery and to be used again. The torpedo was set to run deep so that it would pass under the target ship. If it was to strike a hull, there was a good chance that it would receive more damage than it would inflict on the ship.

During early 1941, Crail played host to a detachment of 812 Squadron, operating the Swordfish, and a few days later, on January 23, a handful of Albacores from 828 Squadron. Flying training was severely hampered at the time by heavy snowfalls, but Crail's tarmac runways were relatively easy to keep clear. Airfields such as Drem, with grass runways, were struggling to operate so, on February 22, the Hurricanes of 43 Squadron were moved to Crail. The Royal Navy were used to running things their way at Crail and the activities of an operational fighter squadron were alien to them. During 43 Squadron's first scramble from Crail, the RAF pilots sent the resident ratings flying and then took off without permission, cross wind and in tight formation. Senior staff at Crail were unimpressed and ordered that the RAF should cease such dangerous flying immediately. By March 1, the weather improved and the Hurricanes made the short flight to their home airfield across the Forth. This would be the only time that the airfield would support an RAF fighter squadron.

Keeping with the tradition of naming its shore bases after birds, Crail was commissioned as HMS Jackdaw on October 1, 1940. (via Martyn Chorlton)

The airfield would provide a useful emergency landing ground for all. A Blenheim from 107 Squadron based at Leuchars found sanctuary at Crail when it crash-landed with engine trouble on March 18. Outbound for Convoy duty, the crew of the twin-engined aircraft was all unhurt.

The Albacore joins in

A new Albacore unit was formed at Crail on April 1, 1941. 831 Squadron, under the command of Lt Cdr P L Mortimer, was created as a torpedo spotter reconnaissance squadron, equipped with twelve Albacore Is. After working up at Crail, the squadron moved to Machrihanish for weapons training on August 26 on to HMS *Indomitable*.

Another long term resident at Crail arrived from Donibristle on June 1, 1941. 770 Squadron, a Fleet Requirements Unit (FRU) arrived with four Blackburn Roc Is under the command of Lt H E R Torin. Two of these aircraft were employed as target tugs, the others were used for target marking. Blackburn Skuas swelled the unit from October followed by a couple of Percival Proctors before the year's end.

Throughout the remainder of 1941, two Albacore units, 820 and 828 Squadron plus two Swordfish units, 819 and 823 Squadron were resident for a few weeks at a time at Crail. The latter was reformed at Crail on November 1 as a TBR unit with nine Swordfish. Before working up, the squadron moved to Fraserburgh on December 6. 819 Squadron, which arrived from Lee-on-Solent, Hampshire on December 10 was to remain at Crail slightly longer. Training began almost immediately with the focus on torpedo dropping and night flying. Poor weather in January 1942 almost wiped the squadron out when six of the nine Swordfish on strength were damaged in a severe gale. The squadron attempted to leave Crail on January 26 but bad weather halted the move until the following day, when the squadron moved to Twatt in the Orkneys.

The Swordfish of 833 Squadron followed on February 5, 1942. Only formed the previous December, the intention was to deploy the unit to the ill-fated HMS *Dasher*. After training at

Fairey Albacores of 785/786 Squadron are prepared for another practice torpedo drop in the Firth of Forth. (via Ray Sturtivant)

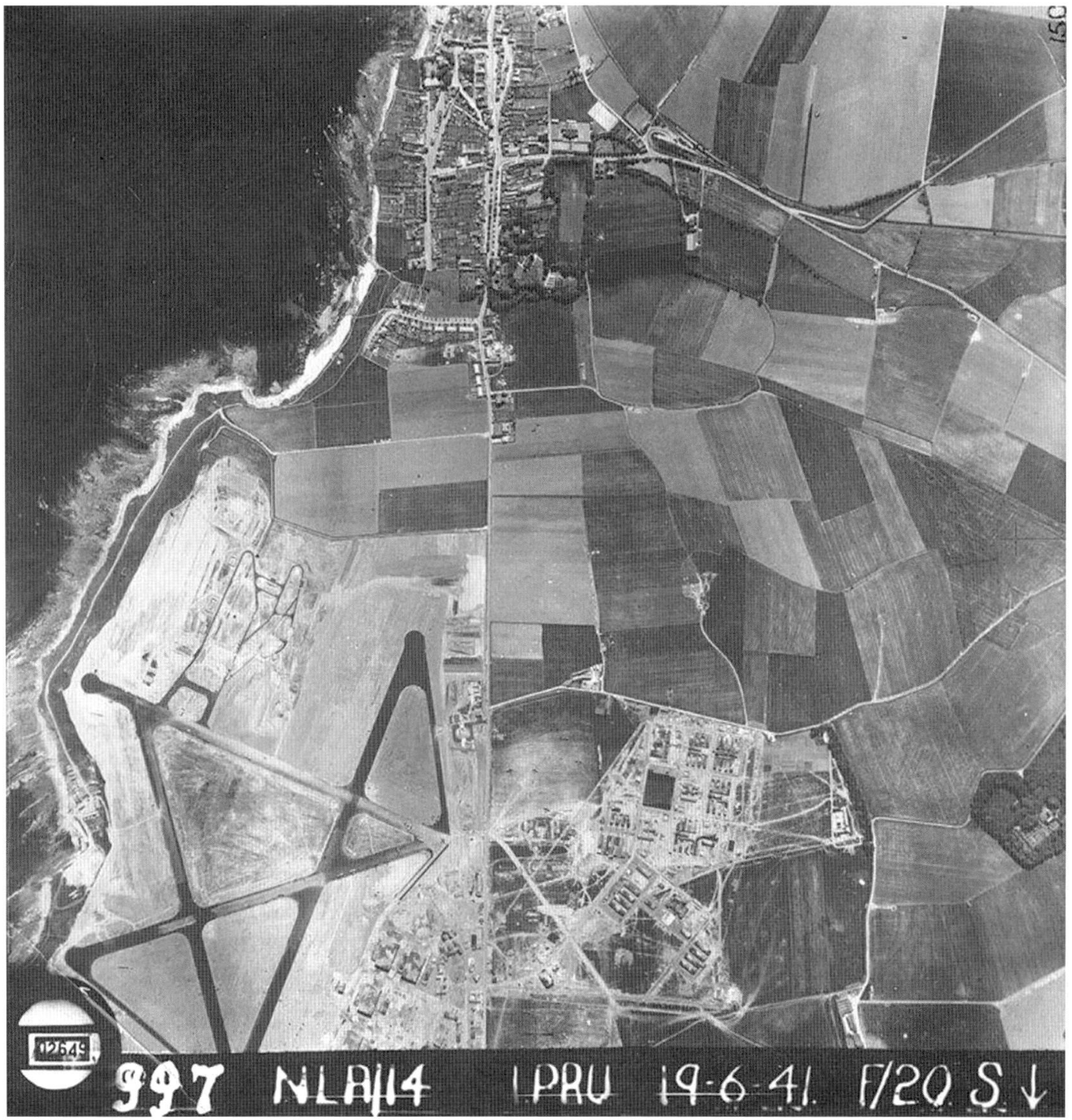

Aerial view of Crail taken on June 19, 1941 by 1PRU shows a typical naval-designed airfield with short, narrow, multiple runways, one of which would always face into the wind. (via Martyn Chorlton)

Crail, the squadron continued to work-up at Hatston and Machrihanish before embarking on HMS *Biter* and service in North African skies. The day before 833 Squadron's departure, another Swordfish unit arrived at Crail. 822 Squadron, under the command of Mjr A R Burch, was a TBR unit equipped with nine Swordfish Is. Destined to serve on HMS *Biter* before the carrier had returned to Britain, the squadron was re-equipped at Crail with the Albacore I. A brief work-up on their new aircraft was achieved at Crail before moving the short distance to Donibristle and eventual service aboard HMS *Furious*.

At nearby Dunino, the airfield's undulating grass runways were not coping well with periods of heavy rain. To aggravate the situation, the resident unit 309 (Polish) Squadron was re-equipping with the North American Mustang. The American fighter was not coping well with state of Dunino and it was

Swordfish I, P3993 '22' carrying out a practice torpedo drop in the Firth of Forth in late 1941. The aircraft first served with 823 Squadron, then 820 Squadron before joining 785 Squadron at Crail in October 1941. By the following month the aircraft was withdrawn from use and SOC on January 14, 1942. (via Martyn Chorlton)

decided to move 'B' Flt to Crail on June 15, 1942. It was during 309 Squadron's stay at Crail that a very interesting sortie took place.

Enter the Barracuda

From December 1942, both 785 and 786 Squadron began to receive the Fairey Barracuda carrier-based torpedo bomber. Initially, only a handful of Mk Is arrived (of which only 30 were built), fitted with a 1,260hp Merlin engine. The ubiquitous Barracuda II, of which 1,688 were built, quickly replaced the seriously underpowered Mk I. Fitted with a more capable 1,640hp Merlin 32, the first of many Barracuda IIs began to arrive at Crail from April 1943 for 785 Squadron, while the unit continued to operate the Swordfish and Albacore alongside the latest Fairey product. 786 Squadron on receiving their first aircraft retired their Swordfish and Albacores within weeks of the Barracuda arriving. By the war's end, 785 Squadron had over 50 Barracudas on strength and 786 Squadron, a remarkable 80 examples of the single-engined torpedo bomber.

As with virtually all FAA and carrier based aircraft, functionality would always be the priority of general appearance. Very few naval aircraft were pleasing to look at and the Barracuda was no

The Swordfish was a common sight at Crail throughout the Second World War. This one, like so many others, is performing seemingly endless circuits and bumps. (via Martyn Chorlton)

exception. The single engine torpedo bomber of all metal construction carried a three-man crew under a long greenhouse-type canopy. It was fitted with a thick cord shoulder wing, a T shaped tail and a spider-like undercarriage, all of which added nothing to its already unusual appearance. The wing design was heavily dictated by the fit of the Fairey-Youngman dive flaps, which made the aircraft very stable when diving from altitude. Defensive armament was simply a pair of machine guns but the aircraft could carry a variety of underwing stores and a single 1,620lb torpedo.

Torpedo Attack Trainer

Dive-bombing was a new art which needed to be taught to the trainee Barracuda crews. Targets were towed behind ships for the crews to bomb and they were supported by many hours in the classroom and on the many simulator trainers that were available at Crail. One of the most impressive simulators available was the Torpedo Attack Trainer (TAT). The TAT consisted of a huge hemispherical screen, measuring 40ft across, on which were projected the images of enemy ships. The pupil was located in the middle of the room inside a Link trainer facing the screen. Above him was a large rotatable platform fitted with various lamps and an epidiascope, which projected the image of the ship, by using models only a few inches long. As the pupil pilot manoeuvred his simulated aircraft, the ship's position would respond accordingly. Once a torpedo was launched, a white line of light showed the track of it and, if the ship stopped on the line, the instructor would confirm a hit. The various lights and lanterns above the pupil could represent just about any weather condition to add even more realism to the

SWORDFISH UNITS AT CRAIL

785 Sqn	Formed Nov 4, 1940 (satt Dunino); disbanded Mar 1, 1946
786 Sqn	Formed Nov 21, 1940 (satt Dunino); disbanded Dec 21, 1945
811 Sqn	'Fighter Flight' formed Nov 25, 1943; to Stretton Dec 10, 1943
812 Sqn	(Dt 3) from North Coates, Jan 16, 1941 to Mar 2, 1941. From Stretton Jun 28, 1944; to Burscough Sep 7, 1944
816 Sqn	From Machrihanish Apr 17, 1944; to Perranporth Apr 20, 1944
819 Sqn	From Lee-on-Solent Dec 8, 1941; to Twatt Jan 27, 1942
823 Sqn	Reformed Nov 1, 1941; to Fraserburgh Dec 6, 1941
829 Sqn	From St Eval Oct 7, 1940; to HMS *Formidable* Nov 15, 1940
833 Sqn	From Lee-on-Solent Feb 5, 1942; to Hatston Mar 21, 1942
834 Sqn	From HMS *Archer* Oct 31, 1942; to Exeter Feb 9, 1943
836 Sqn	From Machrihanish Sep 24, 1942; to Machrihanish Oct 28, 1942
837 Sqn	From Hatston Dec 30, 1942; 'A' Flt to HMS *Argus* Jan 15, 1943 & 'D' Flt to HMS *Dasher* Jan 22, 1943.

The three-storey control tower dominates the airfield with the unique Aircraft Repair Shed visible in the background. (via Martyn Chorlton)

SWORDFISH LOST WHILE SERVING AT CRAIL & DUNINO

Date	Serial	Squadron	Details
Jan 20, 1941	L2808	785 Sqn	Ditched on torpedo training
Jul 4, 1941	K5987	785 Sqn	FL in sea (Sub Lt J Harris)
Jul 16, 1941	K6001	785/786 Sqn	Crashed (Mid E S Linstead)
Aug 18, 1941	L2836	785/786 Sqn	Written off (Sub Lt D H Dibb)
Oct 12, 1941	L9757	785 Sqn	Caught fire immediately after night take-off from Dunino and crashed into Kippur Wood (Sub Lt E H Archer +)
Oct 22, 1941	K5965	785 Sqn	Crashed (Sub Lt B G Smith)
Dec 20, 1941	L2808	785 Sqn	Ditched on torpedo training sortie (Sub Lt P Haines DoI)
Dec 30, 1941	P4144	785 Sqn	Collided with P4261 during formation training 1m W of Crail village (Sub Lt M G N Crawford +)
Dec 30, 1941	P4261	785 Sqn	Collided with P4144 during formation training 1m W of Crail village (Lt N A F Cheesman DFC +)
Feb 12, 1942	L2727	785 Sqn	Broke formation and collided with another Swordfish and spun into the sea (Lt R K Impey +)
Feb 17, 1942	V4555	786 Sqn	Ditched (Lt H C K Housser RCN)
Feb 20, 1942	L2779	785 Sqn	EF, lost at sea (Sub Lt E A Pope)
Mar 13, 1942	L2755	785 Sqn	Crashed (Sub Lt I M Bunker)
Mar 18, 1942	K8360	785 Sqn	Lost in poor weather, FL, crashed at Worthy Down (Sub Lt J P Fournier RCN)
Mar 22, 1942	V4556	786 Sqn	Crashed night flying (Sub Lt E F Pratt)
Apr 2, 1942	L2783	786 Sqn	Flew into sea during torpedo training, S of Elie Ness, Fife (Sub Lt K Stocks +)
May 5, 1942	V4510	786 Sqn	Flew into sea during torpedo training off Elie Ness (Sub Lt R S McKay +)
Jul 28, 1942	DK676	786 Sqn	Ditched after pulling out of dive to late (Sub Lt A J Stammers)
Aug 7, 1942	K6003	786 Sqn	EF, ditched (Mid H B Gainey)
Oct 30, 1942	V4440	786 Sqn	EF, ditched (Sub Lt T J Harris)
Nov 23, 1942	V4635	785 Sqn	EF whilst low flying over sea (Sub Lt J C Baltu)
Late 1942	L9730	786 Sqn	Crashed Glen Callatar, Angus
Jan 24, 1943	V4445	785 Sqn	Hit water during low- flying practice and broke up (Sub Lt R I Currie)
Jan 27, 1943	L2796	785 Sqn	Ditched on ALT exercise (Sub Lt D J Kordek +)
Feb 2, 1943	DK761	785 Sqn	Low flying practice over the sea, u/c hit water and aircraft sank (Sub Lt P G Comber)
Mar 23, 1943	W5840	785 Sqn	Ditched 323¡ off May Island (Mid H L Byatt +)
Apr 13, 1943	K5953	785 Sqn	Run into by Fulmar X8763 which had swung off the runway on take-off (3+ 2 injured)
May 3, 1943	L7676	785/786 Sqn	EF following fuel pump failure (Sub Lt B R Q Bell)
Jun 16, 1943	L7640	785/786 Sqn	Hit sea during ALT exercise (Sub Lt G I Smith)

Jul 28, 1943	DK745	785/786 Sqn	Ditched trying to avoid another aircraft after its lights were mistaken for landing lights (Sub Lt W D R Cattanach)
Aug 26, 1943	DK715	785/786 Sqn	Crashed into sea during low-flying exercise (Sub Lt A N Brinson +)
Oct 9, 1943	V4597	785 Sqn	ALT, pulled out to late and hit sea (Mid A C T Rowe-Evans)
Oct 22, 1943	P4200	785 Sqn	EF in formation at night, FL, crashed, BO
Dec 10, 1943	V4331	785 Sqn	EF, ditched after ALT (Mid N B Cox)
Feb 19, 1944	L2752	785/786 Sqn	Crashed on top another Swordfish during night ADDL; both aircraft wrecked

exercise. A separate lantern fitted under the Link trainer could even replicate various water effects from a millpond sea to large waves. By now, operational training consisted of seven weeks at Crail, which involved learning to drop torpedoes, followed by three weeks deck-landing training to Royal Navy standards at Arbroath.

Swordfish units keep coming

Albacore and Swordfish squadrons continued to pass through Crail during late 1942. 786 Squadron lost one of its valued and highly experienced instructors on November 5. Lt H de G Hunter DSC was demonstrating a practice torpedo attack in Albacore I N4357 only moments before crashing into the Firth of Forth. Lt Hunter had earned his DSC when he was piloting one of 14 Swordfish from HMS *Ark Royal* which disabled the *Bismarck* in May 1941. The repeated attacks by the Swordfish allowed HMS *Dorsetshire* to finish the German battleship off with a single torpedo.

A third permanent unit joined 785, 786 and 770 Squadron on March 5, 1943. 778 Squadron, a Service Trails Unit squadron, brought its collection of aircraft from Arbroath, all under the command of Lt Cdr H J F Lane. Originally formed at Lee-on-Solent in September 1939, the role of the unit was to carry out service trials on all new types of naval aircraft entering service during 1941 and 1942. This included early marks of the Seafire, the Chesapeake, Kingfisher and the Barracuda plus any equipment supporting these aircraft types. The latter, carried out at Crail, included testing aerial mines and flame floats. These were designed to ignite on contact with the water. 778 Squadron was also the first unit to bring the Grumman Avenger to the airfield. It was also the first unit to receive the big American-built torpedo bomber, back in 1942. The Avenger was popular aircraft with its crews and was one of the most stable platforms ever built for the delivery of a torpedo. Out of the 9,839 built, 958 of them served with the FAA from 1943 onwards, with many seeing action in the Far East.

The Barracuda was already a common site at Crail by late 1943, but it was not until October 18 that the first operational squadron arrived. 810 Squadron, under the command of Lt Cdr A J B Forde, arrived from the aircraft carrier HMS *Illustrious* after serving in the Mediterranean. The unit did not stay long and moved to Machrihanish for a weapons training refresher course before re-embarking on HMS *Illustrious* in late November.

811 Squadron, whose main equipment was the Swordfish, formed a new Fighter Flight at Crail on November 25, 1943. Using the American-built Grumman Wildcat IV for the new flight, the unit departed for Stretton, Lancashire on December 10, becoming the last Swordfish unit to serve at Crail.

Altogether over 150 buildings remain in generally good condition at Crail, not to mention all of the runways, taxiways and dispersals. This makes Crail the best-preserved disused airfield in Scotland, possibly ranking as one of the most impressive in Great Britain as well. (via Martyn Chorlton)

Chapter 8

Channel Operations

16 Group, Coastal Command

On July 17, 819 Squadron was attached to 16 Group, Coastal Command, initially based at Langham before moving to Bircham Newton on August 6. Operating at night, it undertook mine-laying sorties as well as strikes against E-boats and shipping in the English Channel and southern North Sea, transferring its work further south on moving to Thorney Island on September 23 and eventually leaving 16 Group for Hatston on October 28. 811 Squadron performed similar tasks, also with

16 Group, working out of Bircham Newton from August 6, then from Thorney Island between October 31 and December 12. Two other squadrons to be attached to 16 Group, both on September 7 for similar duties, were 812 and 816 Squadrons, the former at Docking and the latter at Thorney Island. 812 Squadron moved to Bircham Newton on October 8, and then left for Hatston on 3 November, while 816 left Thorney Island tor Machrihanish on 30 December.

Attached to Fighter Command from August 23 was 841 Squadron, which began operations against E-boats and enemy shipping in the Dover Strait. Based as a lodger with the 11 Group at Manston, it was mainly equipped with Albacores but had a small number of Swordfish attached. From time to time detachments were sent to Fighter Command stations at Tangmere, Coltishall and Exeter for operations in other areas. On March 29, 1943 a squadron Swordfish bombed a line of E-boats

Swordfish IIs of 816 Squadron from St Merryn carry out a practice RP attack in July 1944. During this period the unit became very adept at attacking E-boats in the English Channel. (via Ray Sturtivant)

816 Squadron aircrew being briefed for another anti-E-boat patrol from St Merryn in July 1944. The unit operated the Swordfish I and II from October 1939 to August 1944. (via Ray Sturtivant and P. Snow)

about 50 miles north-east of Happisburgh at 0113hrs, claiming to have damaged one of them. On December 1, 1943 the squadron was disbanded, its task and Albacores being then handed over to the Canadian-manned 415 Squadron. By that time the Albacores and Swordfish had made a total of 99 night attacks.

Several Swordfish squadrons were attached to 16 Group early in 1943. 825 Squadron had moved on December 14 1942 to Thorney Island for night mine-laying and anti-E-boat and anti-shipping strikes and was joined in this task on January 1, 1943 by 836 Squadron. 825 Squadron had a detachment of four aircraft at Exeter from December 30, but this was withdrawn on February 1, 1944 when the squadron was replaced at Thorney Island by 833, 834 Squadron taking over at Exeter. By April all had been withdrawn, though 816 was attached to Exeter from 20 May to 25 June.

Tom Mogford was with 833 Squadron at this time, and recalls:

'Doubtless many TAGs served with squadrons lent to the RAF for various tasks. I had two sessions with Coastal Command, the second of which was, as far as I know, unique in the length of time that an entire naval air squadron was loaned to the RAF. Life during that period was so totally different from anything that we knew in the Navy.

'After *Indomitable* and a spell at Lee, I was drafted early in 1943 to RAF Thorney Island to join 833 Squadron, Stringbags of course. Mine-laying was the main nocturnal occupation at Thorney, the idea being to creep up to the harbour entrance, usually Cherbourg or Le Havre, drop the thing and push off as quickly and quietly as possible, secure in the knowledge that the minesweepers would be out bright and early in the morning to take care of it. After a few weeks we moved down to RAF St Eval, where there was some talk of mining the Brest area, but the idea came to nothing and so we were on our way back to the Navy.'

E-Boat hunting

On 20 May 1943, 816 Squadron moved to Exeter and operated under 10 (Fighter) Group, carrying out anti E-boat patrols. On the night of May 30/31 one of its aircraft bombed and machine-gunned three E-boats travelling south-south-east at 30kts, some 35 miles east-south-east of Start Point, but was unable to observe whether there were any results. On the night of June 6/7 two aircraft attacked around eight E-boats off the French coast but were again unable to tell whether their bombs had any effect. The Squadron left on June 25 for Scotland to work up for escort carrier duty on Atlantic convoys.

Claims made at the time by the naval TSR squadrons involved in this work turned out in retrospect to be somewhat exaggerated. Eleven E- and R-boats were claimed sunk and eight damaged between January 1 and June 15, 1943, but a post-war examination of German records revealed that only three E-boats had been sunk during that period, S74 scuttled after a Beaufighter attack and S75 by a Spitfire, both in the North Sea, and S121 in the Western Channel area by an unspecified aircraft, possibly from Exeter.

By the spring of 1944, British and American forces had built up sufficiently in the United Kingdom for the long-awaited invasion of Europe to become a reality. The Royal Navy would have a major part to play, especially in the initial landings, and the FAA was to be given several vital tasks. In preparation, four RAF bases on the South Coast were taken over during April and May by General Reconnaissance Wings of Coastal Command, whose units included FAA Avenger and Swordfish squadrons which would be land-based for several months. For operations in the English Channel, 155 and 157 Wings flew from, respectively, Manston and Hawkinge. 155 Wing was basically a Beaufighter squadron, but it also included the Avengers of 848 Squadron and the Swordfish of 819, whilst 157 Wing had the Avengers of 854 and 855 Squadrons, these being later replaced by 819 Squadron Swordfish and

A German E-boat, also known as a Schnellboot or S-Boot, which basically meant a fast boat, which it certainly was – capable of speeds of over 40kts, these wooden hull craft were very difficult to hit.

Five Swordfish Is of 825 Squadron, led by Lt Cdr R W Slater DSC pictured operating out of Thorney Island in January 1943. The unit carried out mine-laying, anti-E-boat and anti-shipping strikes until mid-March 1943.

119 Squadron RAF Albacores and Swordfish. In the south-west, Harrowbeer was used by the Swordfish of 838 Squadron in 156 Wing and Perranporth by the Swordfish of 816 Squadron and the Avengers of 849 and 850 Squadrons.

Operating off the coasts of Belgium, France and Holland, the aircraft executed a considerable number of shipping strikes and attacks were made on E-boats and R-boats, in addition to anti-submarine sorties and other varied tasks. 838 Squadron, which moved south from Machrihanish to Harrowbeer on April 20 under the command of Lt Cdr J M Brown DSC, had a traumatic start to its activities. Its first operation was on the night of April 30/[May] 1 when its Swordfish IIs were detailed to attack with RPs a beached *Elbing*-class destroyer on Ile Vierge, which had previously been attacked during the day by RAF fighters. The Operations Record Book of 156 (General Reconnaissance) Wing records the outcome:

'30 April-1 May. Aircraft A, B, C, F, G, H, L, M, S, T and L were detailed to attack with RPs a destroyer in position 48°40'N 4°26'W, though this position was to be amended if consultation with ADGB Intelligence (whose aircraft had been attacking the same target in the afternoon of April 30) made it desirable. This was done, and a position 48°36'N 4°36'W was given to the crews, unfortunately as events proved, for the ship reported in that position was in fact an M class minesweeper and not the *Elbing*-class destroyer, and the surrounding flak was more intense than it would have been at the original position.

'The first aircraft, A, took off at 2215/30 APR, piloted by the Squadron Commander, Lt Cdr J Brown, followed at five-minute intervals by the other eleven aircraft. Only B (Sub Lt H Van Staverin) and M (Sub Lt D J Donovan) succeeded in identifying and attacking the target, though results were unobserved. Considerable flak, bad visibility and 10/10ths cloud, sometimes with base at 400ft,

An 819 Squadron Swordfish from Manston lays a smokescreen for the benefit of Allied shipping during the Normandy landings in June 1944. (via Ray Sturtivant and G. L. P. Steer)

hampered operations. Of the other aircraft, one attacked a fire in the target area, another attacked a searchlight and gunpost, a third went for a dark shape in the mouth of the estuary and a fourth attacked two gunposts and a line of roofs suggesting a factory. Seven aircraft returned to base between 0140/1 May and 0229hrs. Two landed at other stations and three failed to return. The missing crews were F (Sub Lt I L R Wilson, Sub Lt E T Clark and PO A Rockley), G (Sub Lt L F Hayward, Sub Lt D J Hanson and L/A B L Rowntree) and K (Sub Lt S F Such, Lt J B Cook and PO R C Grapes).'

After this rather disastrous start, further patrols were mostly uneventful, the only other loss being a non-operational one on May 18 when Sub-Lt D J Donovan crashed during RP practice on the Treligga range, fortunately without suffering serious injury. The squadron eventually left Harrowbeer three months later.

No escape from ASV

Meanwhile seven aircraft of 819 Squadron moved to Manston from Lee-on-Solent on April 18, a further four aircraft arriving two days later. The Squadron's Swordfish had the advantage of new ASV Mk X radar in radomes under their fuselages, enabling the operators to have a panoramic display of a wide area of coastline and any ships present. It was destined to spend a longer period on this type of work than any other FAA squadron. Various patrols were flown, and some attacks were made on E- or R-boats. On the night of May 19/20, E-boat S87 was reported scuttled 2½ miles off Ostend after an air attack by 819 Squadron, and on the night of May 20/21 'B/819' sighted six wakes, thought to be of E-boats, and attacked with bombs, causing large explosions and showers of sparks. Fires could still be seen burning when the aircraft was fifteen miles on its homeward course. The squadron were afterwards credited with sinking a 200-ton ferry barge off Dieppe. Three nights later they sank a similar vessel of around 250 tons off Calais. On the night of May 30 'P/819' attacked ten or eleven E/R-boats with bombs and obtained a hit on one of them, which was left in flames, other bombs scoring near misses. On D-Day the squadron was given the task of laying a smokescreen over the Allied invasion fleet, commencing at 1518hrs that afternoon, and further such flights were made as required.

Delivered from Blackburn Aircraft on April 4, 1944, NF374 'NH-M' was delivered to 119 Squadron at Bircham Newton on January 17, 1945. The purposeful looking Swordfish gave good service but once the war came to an end the aircraft was scrapped at Barton on June 8, 1945.

On June 27 'X/819', under Swingate control, sighted five motor vessels near the centre of the Strait of Dover. The aircraft attacked and a heavy explosion was seen, followed by a large pall of smoke over the position of the centre ship of the starboard echelon. As the Swordfish departed the scene, the air gunner reported that he could see only four ships and wakes after the attack, though a later examination of German records found no evidence of a sinking.

On October 1, the squadron was withdrawn to Bircham Newton, and activities there appear to have been less intense, but a detachment of 819 Squadron began to operate in Belgium at the end of that month, based initially at St Croix before moving to Maldeghem on November 11, then on December 14 to Knocke-le-Zoute, where it was joined by the remainder of the squadron on February 26, 1945.

Biber hunting

On November 20, 1944, 838 and 842 Squadrons commenced anti-submarine patrols in the central area of the English Channel, the former for a second spell on this work, operating from Thorney Island until disbanding on February 3 and January 15 1945 respectively.

Swordfish were also used by 119 Squadron. This unit had re-formed in 155(GR) Wing at Manston on July 19 1944, initially equipped with Albacores. On August 9 it moved to Swingfield and joined 819 Squadron, which had arrived the previous day, and also became part of 157(GR) Wing. Activities were anti-shipping patrols, especially against E- and R-boats operating along the Dutch coast, and on October 29 it moved to Knocke-le-Zoute, where midget submarines were added to its targets. These were reportedly of two types, the two-seater *Seehund* or Type 27 and the single-seater *Biber*. The latter had a surface range of only 70 nautical miles and a maximum endurance of 72 hours, it being restricted to inshore passage to its operational area at the approaches to the Scheldt. The submarines were based in Dutch ports and threatened the safety of Allied convoys. They usually left their bases shortly after nightfall and made the outward journey under cover of darkness; they were normally only found in daylight when caught still making the hazardous journey back to base.

Early in 1945, 119 Squadron began to exchange its Albacores for new Swordfish IIIs fitted with ASV Mk XI, the first two machines arriving from the UK for training purposes on January 5 and the last

Albacore leaving on January 22. When fully equipped, the new aircraft made a number of attacks on midget submarines and other vessels. On February 26, during an anti-shipping patrol, 'NH-A', piloted by Canadian Flt Lt E A Richardson with Flt Lt G Goodman operating the radar set, made a diving attack at 2045hrs on five unidentified vessels in position 51°59'N 5°01'E, but the crew were unable to observe the results, if any. However, 'NH-E', crewed by Flt Lt J D Hall and Fg Off B H L Blake, was alerted, and this aircraft spotted five E/R boats, first on radar and then visually, in position 51°58'N 3°38'E, and at 2110hrs attacked with three bombs. The results were again unobserved, and five minutes later the crew dropped the remaining bomb, which undershot.

The squadron suffered its first Swordfish loss on March 9 when 'NH-R' (Flt Lt F G Sutton and Fg Off R P Radford) failed to return from a night operation. Two nights later 'NH-U' (Fg Off A O Corbie and Fg Off P O Donnell) sighted the cupola of a midget submarine at 1825hrs in position 51°48'N 3°31'E. The enemy vessel surfaced as the aircraft circled at 300ft to attack, its first 250lb depth charge overshooting by about 30yds. The second attack, from the same height, undershot. The submarine meanwhile continued on its course, but after a third attack, which again undershot, it turned sharply to port though stayed on the surface. The remaining depth charge was then dropped in a fourth attack, and this time a plume of water shot up and the target was not seen again. After about three minutes a large oil streak developed, but there was no certainty that the submarine had been destroyed, so 'NH-R' (Sqn Ldr N Williamson, the CO, with Fg Off J F Gardiner), which was in the vicinity, was homed to the position. Flame floats had been dropped by 'NH-H', and four 250lb MC were dropped between the floats and across patches of black oil which were seen. There was no further sign of the target vessel.

The following afternoon 'NH-L' (Plt Off A E Coles and Flt Sgt R Street) sighted a stationary *Biber* at 1640 in position 51°52'N 3°46'E. They attacked with two 250lb depth charges, one landing only about ten feet from the target, which rose in the water and then started to sink. A second attack was made with one depth charge and the midget submarine disappeared, leaving an oil patch on the surface. Just over an hour later 'NH-R' (Sqn Ldr N Williamson and Flt Lt D G Matkin) carried out an attack on a

A forlorn looking NF119 'X', named *Black Mischief*. On February 3, 1945, its pilot, Sub Lt Chambers had to avoid another aircraft and stalled, with the aircraft's undercarriage catching a boundary fence at Knocke-le-Zoute. Transported to Worthy Down for storage, the aircraft was not repaired and like so many other Swordfish, was scrapped at Barton in June 1945. (via Ray Sturtivant and A. R. Wadham)

819 Squadron Swordfish III, complete with ASV and 250lb bombs under the wings pictured at Biggin Hill on detachment on September 29/30, 1944. The aircraft only served with 819 Squadron until March 1945. (*Aeroplane*)

Biber with fairly similar results at 51°47'N 3°42'E. Three attacks were made from 50ft, the two depth charges dropped on the first run-in slightly overshooting, but direct hits were claimed with each of the other two. The submarine then disappeared, leaving oil patches and wreckage in the area.

On April 5 'NH-O' (Flt Lt W G Barnett DFC and Fg Off A W Bermel, both Canadians) were on patrol when they saw a B-24 Liberator explode in mid-air. A trigger-happy gunner of another B-24 then fired a burst at them, fortunately without effect, and they made a hasty retreat.

Aircraft 'NH-F' (Plt Off H P L Goundry and Plt Off J Templeton DFC) was scrambled on April 12 to search for a *Biber* reported seen about 40 miles north of the base. At 1510hrs they sighted two *Bibers* in position 51°54'N 3°17'E, one stationary on the surface and the other just surfacing about 50yds away. The first *Biber* apparently attempted to submerge, but its conning tower was still visible when the aircraft attacked with all four of its depth charges. The stick fell between the two *Bibers*, the first being blown out of the water and left stationary on the surface. The second one was not seen again.

Following VE-Day. the Squadron ceased activities. Returning to Bircham Newton on 22 May, it was disbanded three days later, the aircraft then departing for Barton to be broken up.

Chapter 9

Fighting the U-Boats!

1940

April 13, 1940, U-64 (2 Flotille)

The first U-boat to be sunk by an aircraft during the Second World War took place during the Second Battle of Narvik, Norway on April 13, 1940. As Vice-Admiral W J Whitworth KCB, DSO on board HMS *Warspite* approached Ofot Fjord, he decided to launch the ship's seaplane, Swordfish L9767 'C8/B' of 700 Squadron flown by P/O F C Rice, Lt Cdr W L M Brown and LAC M G Pacey. At 1152hrs the Swordfish was airborne in poor weather conditions while a force of ten Swordfish from HMS *Furious* found a small window of opportunity in the conditions to attack a group of enemy destroyers without success.

Meanwhile Rice in L9767 continued his patrol into Herjangs Fjord where visibility improved to six miles. It was then that the Swordfish crew came across U-64, under the command of Kptlt Georg-Wilhelm Schulz at anchor, just 50yds from a jetty at Bjerkvik in position 68.29N, 17.30E. Without hesitation, Rice began his attack by diving to 300ft and dropping a pair of 250lb bombs. The first fell directly onto the bows of U-64 and the second either struck the side of the U-boat or came very close. The TAG, LAC Pacey opened fire as they swooped over the U-boat which managed to briefly return fire, causing some damage to the floatplane. It was all over for U-64 very quickly; within

It was an unassuming Swordfish seaplane, like this example, which claimed the title of being the first aircraft to sink a U-boat during the Second World War. (via Martyn Chorlton)

30 seconds the U-boat had sunk but 38 of the 46 crew managed to escape with their lives, the casualties most likely being killed when the first bomb struck.

The day was not over for Rice and his crew, who later reported the position of three German destroyers in Rombaks Fjord. These were later intercepted by Whitworth's force, leaving the *Giese* and *Roeder* ablaze. More enemy ships were called in during Rice's eventful sortie and another German destroyer was forced to run aground during action with HMS *Hero* and *Forrester* before it was finished off by *Warspite* and two remaining 250lb bombs from L9767.

Whitworth later reported that the use of L9767 had been '… invaluable. I doubt if ever a ship-borne aircraft has been used to such good purpose as it was in this operation.' Once the day was over, the Royal Navy could claim eight German destroyers and one U-boat sunk without loss to any British surface ship. Having been in the air for over four hours that day, Rice and Brown were awarded the DSC, while the equally deserving LAC Pacey received no such accolade.

1941

November 30, 1941, U-96 (7 Flottille)

At 2235hrs a Swordfish from 812 Squadron, operating from RAF North Front (Gibraltar) caught U-96 on the surface trying to enter the Mediterranean via the Straits of Gibraltar. Under the command of Kptlt Heinrich Lehmann-Willenbrock, U-96 had left St Nazaire on October 27 and only a few days later had opened its account by sinking the Dutch 5,998-ton merchant ship, *Bennekom*, which was part of convoy OS-10.

The Second Battle of Narvik underway as viewed from L9767. (via Martyn Chorlton)

U-288 under attack from an 819 Squadron Swordfish and a Grumman Avenger of 846 Squadron, on April 3, 1944.

It was a clear night aided by a fair amount of moonlight, although the U-boat was first sighted by ASV six miles away and visually within two miles. The Swordfish attack forced U-96 to crash dive with some damage and the boat remained below the surface until 0445hrs on December 1. This experience was later related by the German war correspondent Lothar-Günther Buchmein as part of his bestselling novel *Das Boot*. U-64 crawled back into St Nazaire for repairs on December 6.

December 2, 1941, U-558 (1 Flotille)
In similar fashion to U-96, the U-boat U-558 under the command of Günther Krech was caught on the surface trying to enter the Mediterranean. Once again it was an ASV-equipped Swordfish from 812 Squadron that spotted the boat, but on this occasion, the aircraft managed to also call in a pair of Royal Navy surface escort ships. It is not clear if the Swordfish managed to deliver a successful attack but depth charges did cause extensive damage to U-558, which was forced to return to Brest for repairs after only being at sea for 14 days.

December 15, 1941, U-432 (3 Flotille)
812 Squadron's good run of discovering U-boats trying to enter the Mediterranean continued on December 15, when U-432, under the command of Kptlt Heinz-Otto Schultze, was caught on the surface 34 miles northwest of Trafalgar. On this night, though the ASV failed to pick up the enemy boat, the vessel was spotted visually within half a mile. A depth charge attack was carried out at 0540hrs which caused sufficient damage to force the U-boat to end its war patrol and return to La Pallice for repairs.

View from an 811 Squadron Swordfish on approach to HMS Biter in 1943. The squadron operated from escort carrier, on and off, from February 1943 to August 1944. Originally laid down as a merchant ship in Pennsylvania, the carrier served the Royal Navy from 1942 to 1945 when it was sold to the French and renamed as the *Dixmunde*. Retired in 1956, it was sunk as a target ship in 1966. (*Aeroplane*)

December 16, 1941, U-569 (3 Flotille)

812 Squadron continued to harry the U-boats when another was attacked nine miles west of Cape Spartel off the Moroccan coast. The victim on this occasion was U-539 (under the command of Hans-Peter Hinsch) which had only left St Nazaire six days earlier. Once again, it was while attempting to enter the Mediterranean that the 812 Squadron Swordfish picked up the U-boat on its ASV. At 2119hrs the attack began, but the Swordfish had to close to within a quarter of a mile of U-569 before the depth charges were dropped. Frustratingly for the Swordfish crew, only serious damage was caused and, like the U-boats before it, the vessel managed to return to its home port for repairs.

December 19, 1941, U-202 (1 Flotille)

Often claimed to have been an attack made by an 819 Squadron, which was based at Crail at the time, this action was again carried out by an 812 Squadron Swordfish from North Front. The vessel on the receiving end of the depth charges was U-202 under the command of Kptlt Hans-Heinz Linder out of Brest. At 2141hrs, 2½ miles west of Cape Spartel, the Swordfish crew dropped a depth charge ahead of a large swirl which, unbeknown the crew of the biplane, had caused enough damage to convince Linder to return to Brest for repairs.

December 21, 1941, U-451 (3 Flotille)

812 Squadron's perseverance finally paid off on December 21, 1941 when U-451 was attacked off Tangier, 13 miles from in Cape Spartel in position 35.55N, 06.08W. On only its fourth war

Right: **Kptlt Heinrich Lehmann-Willenbrock, the commander of U-96 pictured at St Nazaire.**

Below: **842 Squadron, operating from HMS** *Fencer* **carried out a host of attacks on U-boats, not all successful. Sub Lt B F Vibert was returning from such an encounter on December 20, 1943 in LS191 'A'.**

U-558, under the command of Günther Krech. The U-boat was damaged by an ASV-equipped 812 Squadron Swordfish whilst trying to enter the Mediterranean on December 2, 1941.

patrol, U-451 under the command of KrvKpt Eberhard Hoffman left Lorient on December 15 with orders to enter the Mediterranean.

From North Front, Sub-Lt P McJ Wilkinson took off in Swordfish, V4331 'A' accompanied by his observer, Lt L C Plummer and TAG, L/A H J Oppenheim. It was a very dark moonless night and contact with U-451 was first made by ASV just 3½ miles from the target, which was travelling at 18kts on the surface. Visual confirmation was made at just half a mile and Wilkinson managed to drop three depth charges across the bows of U-451 before it had chance to crash dive. One depth charge, which was set to explode at 25ft, went off directly under U-451, sealing the boat's fate – it sank instantly.

Only U-451's IWO (Intelligence Watch Officer), Oblt Walter Köhler, who was one of four men on the bridge, survived the attack. Köhler later described how they were unaware that an attack was underway, until the depth charges started to fall, because the sound of the U-boat's engines was drowning out the Pegasus engine of the Swordfish. Köhler was rescued, an hour and half later by the corvette HMS *Myosotis*.

This action was the first time a U-boat had been sunk at night and as a result, 812 Squadron not only chalked up its first, well-deserved victory, but Wilkinson and Plummer were awarded the DSC and Oppenheim was awarded the DSM.

1942

January 15, 1942, U-577 (29 Flotille)
Originally credited to a Sunderland from 230 Squadron, the sinking of U-577 was actually carried out by Swordfish, 'G' of 815 Squadron flown by Sub Lt E D Dunkerley, Lt F Walker and L/A Dodwell. The attack took place north-west of Mersa Matruh in position 32.22N, 26.54E.

U-577, under the command of KrvKpt Herbert Schauenburg, was one of the few U-boats that managed to get into the Mediterranean in late December to operate from Messina, Sicily. On only its third war patrol, the U-boat was lost with all 43 hands.

June 2, 1942, U-652 (29 Flotille)

Despite only carrying out eight war patrols, the career of U-652 under the command of Oblt Georg-Werner Fraatz had been a successful one, with 32,285 tons of shipping sunk to its credit. On May 25, 1942, U-652 left Pola (Pula) on the Adriatic coast, but only nine days later was attacked by a 815 Squadron Swordfish and a 203 Squadron Blenheim.

The Swordfish, V7407 'L' was flown by Lt G H Bates, who dropped several depth charges on the U-boat in position 31.55.N, 25.11E in the Gulf of Sollum. The damage caused was severe enough to force Fraatz to scuttle U-652 and, after all 46 crew had safely escaped the U-boat, it was finished off by a single torpedo from U-81.

September 14, 1942, U-589 (11 Flotille)

The next action was the first to involve a Swordfish in the Atlantic Ocean whilst protecting Convoy PQ 18 which was destined to arrive in Russia with the lowest losses recorded so far.

The Swordfish involved this day were from 825 Squadron under the leadership of Lt Cdr S Keane. The aircraft were operating from the escort carrier HMS *Avenger*, commanded by an ex-Swordfish pilot, Cdr A P Colthurst.

The convoy had been under sustained air and U-boat attack since September 12, but two days later, one 825 Squadron Swordfish began to turn the table. At 0940hrs U-589, under the command of KrvKpt Hans-Joachim Horrer, crash-dived after being spotted on the surface in an attempt to escape the slow

HMS *Fencer* was originally built for the US Navy as USS *Croatan*, being commissioned on February 20, 1943. However, under Lend-Lease, the ship was immediately transferred to the Royal Navy the same day to serve as an anti-submarine carrier.

One of several engagements with the enemy by 842 Squadron during early May 1944, whilst operating from HMS *Fencer*.

moving biplane. However, depth charges dropped by the Swordfish forced the U-boat back to the surface and into the sights of HMS *Onslow*, which finished the crippled boat off with the loss of all 44 hands plus four Luftwaffe airmen who had been rescued the day before.

1943

April 25, 1943, U-203 (1 Flotille)

811 Squadron under the command of Lt A S Kennard DSC joined HMS *Biter* in February 1943 with the primary task of performing anti-submarine operations. It was while escorting convoy ONS.4 as part of the 5th Escort Group that 811 Squadron came across its first U-boat on April 23. The boat promptly crash dived before an attack could be carried out but a second sighting on April 25 proofed to be more successful.

The U-boat in question was the highly successful U-203 which was carrying out its eleventh war patrol with Kptlt Hermann Kottman at the helm and had accumulated an impressive total of 111,322 tons of Allied shipping sunk. The U-boat was initially spotted by an 811 Squadron Swordfish, 'L' which, owing to light winds that day was only carrying a pair of depth charges rather than the usual four. U-203 managed to dive approximately 20 seconds before the Swordfish arrived over its position at 55.05N, 42.25W and after dropping its depth charges, marked the position with a Calcium sea marker. No damage is believed to have been caused by the Swordfish attack but prompt action by the Royal Navy destroyer HMS *Pathfinder* which made five depth charge attacks over a two hour period eventually forced the U-203 to the surface before promptly sinking with 10 hands.

This action was the first time a Swordfish had been actively involved in the sinking of a U-boat from an escort carrier.

May 12, 1943, U-89 (9 Flotille)

811 Squadron were in action trying to protect convoy HX.237 which was travelling from New York, bound for Liverpool. At 1232hrs on May 12, Swordfish, HS436 'B' spotted a U-boat on the surface six miles in front of the convoy in position 46.30N, 25.40W. At the same time the destroyer HMS

Broadway and frigate HMS *Lagan* steamed at full speed towards the U-boat. Thirteen minutes later *Broadway* reported that it had seen a pair of U-boats and the Swordfish attacking one of them with depth charges followed with a sea marker to aid the Allied warships. The crew of HS436 then flew back towards *Broadway* to guide the destroyer to the exact spot where they had carried out their attack. Unbeknown to the Swordfish crew, they had inflicted crippling damage on U-89 (under the command of KrvKpt Dietrich Lohmann) which had barely moved by the time *Broadway* arrived above them. *Broadway* laid additional depth charges and at 1447hrs the remains of the U-boat began to rise to the surface; none of the 48 crew survived.

May 23, 1943, U-752 (3 Flotille)
At 1000hrs on May 23, while convoy HX.239 was 750 miles west of Iceland, HMS *Archer* despatched 819 Squadron, Swordfish HS608 'B' flown by Sub Lt H Horrocks, Sub Lt W W N Balkwill and L/A J W Wick on an anti-submarine patrol. Armed with eight rocket projectiles (RPs), the Swordfish was given orders to loiter above the port quarter of the convoy and await further orders. After approximately 15 minutes and in a position 35 miles behind HX.239, a U-boat was spotted on the surface at a range of ten miles. Horrocks turned towards the potential target, skilfully using cloud cover to hide his approach until the Swordfish was within a mile of the U-boat, which was identified as U-752 out of St Nazaire under the command of Kptlt Karl-Ernst Schroeter.

As the Swordfish dived down, Horrocks launched his RPs in pairs, the first from 800yds and the final pair from 200yds – the latter hitting the U-boat below the waterline, approximately 20ft in front of the rudder. U-752 was now unable to dive or keep on an even keel, forcing the crew to fight it out on the surface and hopefully drive the enemy biplane away. The Swordfish wisely withdrew out of range but at

A rather camera-shy vessel throughout its career with the Royal Navy, HMS *Archer* is pictured at Charleston, South Carolina, after its flight was extended in early 1942. A single Swordfish of 834 Squadron can be seen on deck with its wings folded.

the same an 811 Squadron Martlet arrived on the scene, dived down on U-752 and let loose 600 rounds of ammunition into the conning tower which killed Schroeter outright. During this attack, the U-boat's surviving gun crew sheltered behind the conning tower, only to re-appear as U-752 sank beneath them. 29 crew were killed, but 17 men did survive, four of them escaping captivity when they were later rescued by U-91 the same day.

Once again the Swordfish had made history, as this attack was the first time a U-boat had been sunk by RPs and as result both Horrocks and Balkwill were awarded the DSC, and Wick the DSM.

September 12, 1943, U-617 (29 Flotille)
It is not clear what part Swordfish from 833 and 886 Squadrons played in the demise of U-617 off Melilla in position 35.38N, 03.27W, as initial credit is given to a pair of Hudsons from 48 and 233 Squadrons. The U-boat was later finished off by Royal Navy corvette HMS *Hyacinth* and the Australian minesweeper HMAS *Wollongong* after all 49 crew were rescued.

1944

March 4, 1944, U-472 (11 Flotille)

During the twilight hours of March 4, Sub Lt P J Beresford, observer Sub Lt W F Laing and TAG L/A J Beech were on patrol at 3,500ft in their Swordfish, HS641 'B' named *Miss Blandish* of 816 Squadron from HMS *Chaser* which was helping to protect convoy RA.57.

The crew later spotted the wake of U-472, on its first war patrol out of Narvik under the command of Oblt Wolfgang Friedrich von Forstner at a distance of eight miles closing to within ten miles of the convoy. In position 73.05N, 26.40E, *Miss Blandish* closed in for an attack and at a range of 600yds let loose eight RPs in pairs. Unfortunately for Forstner, he ordered an evasive turn to starboard, steering it straight into the path of the RPs which slammed into the U-boat. U-472 continued at full speed on the surface, trailing oil, before coming to halt after briefly issuing return fire towards the Swordfish. In the meantime, Laing had contacted HMS *Onslaught* which closed in on the scene to finish the U-boat off. However, before the destroyer arrived, Forstner found his position to be hopeless as the U-boat could

U-203, a Type VIIC U-boat, leaving Brest with Kptlt Rolf Mützelburg at the helm in August 1942.

U-89, secure in the U-boat pens at La Pallice (La Rochelle) in early April 1943. Only weeks later it was crippled by an 811 Squadron Swordfish in position 46.30N, 25.40W on May 12, 1943.

not dive forcing him to scuttle the vessel. *Onslaught* did fire a few rounds at the crippled U-boat but instead, along with HMS *Orihi*, found itself rescuing 30 survivors from U-472.

Miss Blandish went on to attack two other U-boats after U-472 and is believed to have damaged at least one of them. Beresford and Laing were awarded the DSC for their action that day and Beech received the DSM.

March 5, 1944, U-366 (13 Flotille)

816 Squadron were in action again on March 5 when Sub Lt J F Mason, Sub Lt D Street and L/A Franklin in Swordfish 'F' spotted U-366 through the haze in position 72.10N, 13.45E. Mason manoeuvred with the sun behind them and climbed from 2,300 to 3,000ft with the submarine downwind, completely unaware that they were about to be attacked. Mason entered a gentle dive at a range of two miles and then, once the Swordfish was just a mile away, attacked the U-boat with all eight RPs from a height of 1,200ft. At least three RPs struck U-366 in the conning tower, the crew only responding 30 seconds after the attack with some inaccurate defensive fire. Two minutes after the RPs had struck, the bow of the U-boat began to rise, reaching an angle of 70°, at which point, the vessel slid stern first under the waves. Approximately 30 of the 50-man crew were seen to enter the water without dinghies and as a result all died in the icy water. Once again U-366, under the command of Oblt Bruno Langenberg was on its first war patrol having left Hammerfest only the day before.

Mason and Street were later awarded the DSC for their success and Franklin the DSM.

March 6, 1944, U-973 (5 Flotille)

U-boats continued to harry convoy RA.57, but 816 Squadron also kept up the pressure, achieving success again on March 6. At 0928hrs, Sub Lt L E B Bennett, Sub Lt E W Horsfield and PO C A Vines in Swordfish 'X' spotted U-973 twelve miles from the convoy in position 70.94N, 05.48E. Bennett skilfully closed on the U-boat by making use of a thin layer of cloud to get into a good position before beginning his dive. The Swordfish emerged from the cloud just a mile away from U-973, whose gunners, on this occasion were more vigilant and opened fire with 20mm and 40mm guns. At 800yds, Bennett launched three pairs of RPs, one pair striking the conning tower, while the remainder fell short, although one of these ricocheted off the sea and almost hit one of the gun crews. No significant damage, at first, appeared to have been caused by the attack, but after U-973 performed a few evasive manoeuvres from port to starboard, the stern of the U-boat quickly rose to 60° and the vessel rapidly disappeared below the surface in mass of swirling bubbles and oil. Of the 50 crew on board, approximately 15 were seen to enter the water, but when the destroyer HMS *Boadicea* arrived on the scene only two could be rescued.

U-973 under the command of Oblt Klaus Paepenmöller had a short career; its war patrol out of Trondheim was its second – and last. Bennett and Horsfield received the DSC and Vines the DSM for their actions this day.

March 15, 1944, U-653 (1 Flotille)

A Swordfish contributed to the destruction of U-653, under the command of Oblt Hans-Albrecht Kandler on March 2, on its ninth war patrol, 14 days out of Brest. At 0115hrs, 825 Squadron Swordfish 'A' from HMS *Vindex*, crewed by Lt G Bennett, Sub Lt P S Crouch and NA J J Palmer made an ASV contact with the U-boat in position 53.46N, 24.35W. Depth charges, sea makers and flares were dropped without any result but the aircraft held station until the surface ships HMS *Starling* and *Wild Goose* arrived and took over. By 0305hrs U-653 exploded with the loss of all 51 hands.

April 3, 1944, U-288 (13 Flotille)

Made up of 47 merchant ships, the heavily protected convoy JW.58/RA.58 left Loch Ewe in the north-west Highlands of Scotland on March 27. Forming part of the defence was the increasingly successful 2nd Support Group which included the escort carriers HMS *Activity* with the Swordfish of 819 Squadron on board and HMS *Tracker* carrying the Wildcats and Avengers of 846 Squadron.

U-boats had been attacking the convoy since March 29 but had come off poorly; U-961, U-355 and U-360 had all been sunk by April 3 without loss to the Allies. Swordfish had been in the air from 819 Squadron during all these actions, but it was not until the early hours of April 3 that credit could be given.

Lt S Brilliant DSC, Sub Lt H Chadwick DSC and L/A J Perry DSM took off in Swordfish LS373 'C' from HMS *Activity* at 0312hrs and at 0345hrs spotted a suspected periscope. After dropping a sea marker in the position, the Swordfish crew loitered around the area but nothing more was seen so Brilliant decided to continue their patrol. At 0500hrs the patrol was nearing its conclusion and rather than returning directly to *Activity,* a diversion back to where the marker was dropped was carried out to satisfy the Swordfish crew's curiosity. The diversion paid off, because at 0518hrs U-288, under the command of Oblt Willy Meyer had just surfaced only six miles away. As the Swordfish closed to attack, Avenger 'G' and Wildcat 'Y' closed in on U-288 at the same time and a co-ordinated, combined attack ensued.

The Wildcat attacked first, firing 1,300 rounds at the U-boat, which had decided to fight it out the surface. The Avenger followed, but none of its four depth charges would release, followed by the

Swordfish, which loosed off seven of its eight RPs, all of which are believed to have slammed into U-288. By this time, the submarine was dead in the water and beginning to settle and was finally finished off by a second pass by the Avenger, which managed to release its depth charges. The U-boat blew up seconds later, killing all 49 hands on board.

May 1, 1944, U-277 (13 Flotille)

The action continued around convoy RA.59 during the early hours of May 1 when at 0247hrs, U-277 was spotted in position 73.24N, 15.32E by Sub Lt L G Cooper, Lt R V Barnes and PO K Sutherland in Swordfish LS369 'C' of 842 Squadron.

After shadowing the U-boat for just three quarters of mile, the Swordfish crew was spotted and enemy gun crews opened fire that was returned by Sunderland. At 0307hrs, U-277 under the command of Kptlt Robert Lübsen made the mistake of submerging. Cooper closed on the diving U-boat as fast as he could and dropped a pair of depth charges just before U-277 disappeared. Ten seconds later, there was a large explosion below the surface but it was another 15 minutes before debris began to rise to the surface. The U-boat had no chance of escape; all 50 hands on board were killed.

May 2, 1944, U-674 (11 Flotille)

At 1131hrs the crew of Swordfish LS368 'A' of 842 Squadron, flown by Sub Lt J A Metcalfe, Sub Lt T H Jones and PO J B Shaw spotted a U-boat on the surface in position 70.32N, 04.37E. Approximately six miles away and travelling at between twelve and 15kts, Metcalfe climbed to gain some cloud cover and closed to within 1½ miles of the target. Armed with RPs, Metcalfe dived down towards his quarry firing pairs of rockets at 800, 600, 500 and finally 400yds. No evasive action appeared to have been carried out by the U-boat commander Oblt Harald Muhs and, after being struck by the third and fourth pairs of RPs, the vessel slipped beneath the waves and was never heard from again.

A pair of 813 Squadron Swordfish, operating from HMS *Campania* claimed the last U-boat sunk by the type on December 13, 1944. NF192, 'Q', loaded with eight RPs first joined the squadron in April 1944.

May 2, 1944, U-959 (13 Flotille)

Sub Lt Cooper, Lt Barnes and PO Sutherland were on patrol again during the late afternoon of May 2, this time, flying Swordfish LS284 'K'. At 1630hrs, having taken off from HMS *Fencer* carrying three depth charges in response to a sighting of a U-boat, said vessel was spotted on the surface just eleven minutes after take-off, in position 69.20N, 00.20W. The U-boat was U-959 under the command of Oblt Friedrich Weitz and had left Narvik on May 2, on only its second war patrol.

Approaching out of the sun, Cooper descended from 2,000 to 1,000ft with his Pegasus engine throttled back. Within half a mile of U-959, Cooper dived steeply, levelling out at just 100ft and within 300yds of the unsuspecting U-boat. Once over the conning tower all three depth charges were dropped, straddling the U-boat, with the devices exploding underneath and towards the stern. The Swordfish crew then shadowed the U-boat for a few minutes before U-959 slowed to stop; its bow rose to an angle of 80° and the vessel slid stern first below the waves and sank without trace.

May 6, 1944, U-765 (7 Flotille)

The action that would ultimately claim the scalp of U-765 under the command of Oblt Werner Wendt began at 2242hrs on May 5. The crew of Swordfish NE971 'X' of 825 Squadron operating from HMS *Vindex*, Sub Lt R E Huggins, Sub Lt P T Calcutt and L/A F Smeeton made a strong ASV contact approximately 90 miles from the escort carrier. Running low on fuel, they were forced to return to *Vindex* without making further contact and after jettisoning their depth charges 15 minutes from landing, a U-boat was spotted on surface. The U-boat eventually dived but Huggins and his crew dropped a smoke float to mark the spot which also gave *Vindex* enough time gain a radar fix on the position. Weather conditions began to deteriorate with visibility down to 400yds but Huggins got NE971 safely back down on his carrier, its role in this action now over.

Several other Swordfish were launched to cover the location including 825 Squadron's commanding officer, Lt Cdr F G B Sheffield in Swordfish 'A', in company with Sub Lt J Vallely and CPO M W Dale in NE996 'V'. Despite the poor weather conditions, a square search was initiated, with the frigate HMS *Keats* and later *Bickerton* and *Bligh* also joining in from 0540hrs. At 0605hrs, following a batch of depth charges dropped by HMS *Bligh*, U-765 was forced to the surface just half a mile astern of the frigate. Lt Cdr Sheffield quickly spotted the U-boat – now under intensive accurate fire from the three frigates and also under attack by Vallely in NE996, which was being fired upon by the U-boat as well. Vallely stuck to the task and, at a height of 75ft, two depth charges were dropped, both near the conning tower. U-765 stopped quickly in the water and after briefly settling, the vessel dramatically broke in two with bow and stern pointing at 45° before rapidly sinking in position 52.30N, 28.28W. Eleven survivors were picked up and for their efforts that day, the six aircrew in the Swordfish were all Mentioned in Despatches.

August 22, 1944, U-344 (11 Flotille)

At 0834hrs Swordfish NR857 'X' of 825 Squadron from HMS *Vindex*, crewed by Lt G Bennett and Sub Lt P S Crouch was about to climb into cloud when a U-boat surfacing in position 7454N, 15.26E was spotted only three miles from the aircraft. Bennett immediately dived towards the target, later identified as U-344, commanded by Kptlt Ulrich Pietsch, which had left Bogenbucht on August 3.

At height of 50ft, Bennett dropped three depth charges along the length of the U-boat, although one did not explode immediately because it had got caught up in the deck fittings of U-344 and did not detonate until the boat submerged to a depth of 25ft. Only one survivor was seen in the water. The Swordfish crew attempted to drop a dinghy, but it became tangled in the aircraft's tail wires and was shredded long before it hit the water.

August 24, 1944, U-354 (13 Flotille)

At 0235hrs Sub Lt R J Shaw and Sub Lt A Drysdale in Swordfish NR915 'W' of 825 Squadron spotted what was later identified as U-354 on the surface. After closing to within a mile of the U-boat, defensive fire forced the Swordfish crew to break off and call up the Escort Group. The destroyer, HMS *Keppel* was the first on the scene, the ship distracting the U-boat crew long enough for Shaw to take his opportunity to attack. Shaw straddled submerging U-354 with three pairs of RPs, the last entering the water 100yds ahead of swirling water.

Nothing more was seen of U-354 until 0500hrs when the commander Oblt Hans-Jürgen Sthamer broke surface in full view of the frigate HMS *Loch Dunvegan* and the sloops *Mermaid* and *Peacock*. All three ships then relentlessly dropped depth charges and hunted the U-boat for the next three hours. While no kill was confirmed that day, U-354 never returned to its home base of Narvik.

September 2, 1944, U-394 (11 Flotille)

Yet to open its account, U-394 under the command of Kptlt Wolfgang Borger left Hammerfest on July 27 on only its second war patrol.

Kptlt Heimar Wedemeyer, the commander of U-365 from February 19 to November 11, 1944 saluting the flag of the U-boat at Tromsö.

At 0615hrs a solid H/F D/F fix was made on an unknown target and in response Swordfish NR887 'V' of 825 Squadron, crewed by Lt Cdr F G B Sheffield and Sub Lt J Vallely was directed to position 69.47N, 04.10E. Within five minutes of arriving in the general area, U-394 was spotted on the surface and was clearly in the mood to fight it out with the Swordfish on the surface. Strong defensive fire from U-394 did not deter Sheffield from attacking, at first with four RPs: the first pair falling 300ft short of the U-boat and second only 30ft short. A pair of depth charges were also dropped as the U-boat crashed dived, but neither was observed to explode. Destroyers HMS *Keppel* and *Whitehall* and sloops, *Mermaid* and *Peacock* were directed to the area, which eventually resulted in the conformation that U-394 had been sunk.

December 13, 1944, U-365 (13 Flotille)
The last U-boat to be sunk by a Swordfish during the Second World War was claimed by a pair from 813 Squadron, operating from the escort carrier HMS *Campania*. Very faint signals from a suspected U-boat had been picked up for most of the day by the escort group protecting Convoy JW.62/RA.62 (Operation *Acumen*). At 1531hrs, *Campania* launched Swordfish NR998 'GK' flown by Sub Lt J F Biggins who, in position 71.09N, 08.26E, spotted a surfaced U-boat and attacked with three depth charges just as the enemy crash dived.

The enemy was U-365, being commanded for the first time by Oblt Diether Todenhagen, a U-boat that was more experienced than most, as it was on its eighth war patrol out of Kilbotn. Biggins also dropped a marker which failed to light and the depth charges seemed to have caused no damage to the U-boat. A few minutes later the U-boat was spotted again having re-surfaced, but Biggins could do nothing more than drop a pair of flares, at which point U-365 began to open fire. At 1555hrs two more Swordfish were despatched from *Campania*, NR974 'GQ' crewed by Sub Lt M W Henley and Lt C D Chapman and NR934 'GL' crewed by Sub Lt W J L Hutchinson and Sub Lt A I Farningham. It was not until 1730hrs that a potential U-boat target appeared on the radar screen of Sub Lt Farningham. Between the two Swordfish, the crews decided that Hutchinson's aircraft would be used to light up the target while Henley's would attack. This was duly carried out with three depth charges, all dropped perfectly at 30ft intervals straddling U-365. The stern of the U-boat then rose to an angle of 45° before sliding down below the waves, leaving a large patch of oil and wreckage behind it. All 50 hands were lost.

Chapter 10

HMS *Argus* – A Tour of Duty on the Old *Hat Box*

A sample from Michael Hill's book, *Duty Free: Fleet Air Arm Days*.

A ship with a long and rich history, HMS *Argus* was originally laid down as ocean liner Conte Rosso for Italy. However, on the outbreak of the First World War, work was suspended and in September 1916 the part-built ship was acquired by the Admiralty. It was then developed into an aircraft carrier, the first ship to be built specifically for this role.

'Smashing totties' & 'wizard popsies'

A spell of leave included several days in London staying at the Brevet Clubs (one in Charles Street, the other round the corner in Chesterfield Street). These small private clubs were the lively haunts (with nearby Shepheards) of aircrew during the war. Bars where you drew your own beer from barrels, dining-rooms with excellent food from the black market and some rather tatty bedrooms made up the two old houses. Since one club was licensed from 11am to 3pm and the other from 3pm to 11pm, it was possible (and probable) to drink all day. One also met attractive young women (the 'smashing totties' and 'wizard popsies' of RAF slang). I became friends with two who had a flat in Cornwall Gardens, South Kensington; one was vaguely married and the other, as it happened, was a former girlfriend of 'Buster', the Wing Leader.

It was a very easy-going relationship which I resumed whenever I was in London. Staying at their flat I spent many relaxed hours in the Harrington Arms in Gloucester Road and the nearby Strollers

EAST HAVEN, TAYSIDE

N56º31'41", W02º39'21". Between Arbroath and Carnoustie, S of the A92.

Built specifically for the use of the FAA, this compact and well-equipped air station had a short but useful career.

Planned to become HMS *Dotterel*, it was opened as HMS *Peewit* instead on May 1, 1943. The first unit, 767 Squadron, with Swordfish and Albacores, moved in from Arbroath on May 5. 767 Squadron was a DLT squadron that made full use of several training carriers as well as East Haven's deck-like runways.

It was joined by 769 Squadron, also from Arbroath, and a DLT unit with the Swordfish. However, after only a few days, the squadron began to receive Barracudas, although the Swordfish would remain until early 1944. 769 Squadron also carried the additional task of training DLCOs of which it managed to pass out several courses before the task was handed over to a brand new squadron.

731 Squadron was formed here on December 5, 1943, to continue training the DLCOs. The DLCOs were better known as 'batsmen' and to gain experience the circuit was rarely empty of aircraft has pilots carried out dummy deck landings. It was from this type of training that term 'Clockwork Mice' was invented referring to the pilots carrying out endless landings and take offs. Whether it was through boredom or a genuine order to test the batsmen, many pilots used to carry out what can only be described as 'eccentric' flying to make the task as difficult as possible for the DLCO pupil.

731 Squadron's tasking came to an end on November 1, 1945 when it was absorbed into 768 Squadron. The latter unit had arrived from Ballyhalbert on October 25, 1945, equipped with Seafires and Corsairs. It carried out DLT training offshore with detachments on HMS *Ravager* and *Premier* before disbanding on April 16, 1946.

During this period of activity, East Haven had also been home to an Aircraft Handling training unit and a Fire Fighting School before it was paid off on August 14, 1946. It was not long before the land was returned to its original owners and back to agriculture.

Main Features: *Tarmac runways*: QDM 055-235 1,220yds, 009-189 1,060yds, 099-279 1,015yds, 145-325 1,000yds. *Hangars*: 12 60'x70', 12 Storage. *Hardstandings*: 4. *Accommodation*: 1,166 RN, 378 WRNS.

Club. It was in the Harrington one morning that I was introduced to a Captain White, an amiable man in civilian clothes who stood his round and listened politely to my tales of naval life. After he had gone I remarked that he was quite reasonable for a 'brown job'. Didn't you know, they said, highly amused, that he's the captain of *Illustrious* (one of the more famous fleet carriers).

And so to East Haven, a small naval air station on the Scottish coast not far from Carnoustie. This was the training school for 'batsmen' (as Deck Landing Control Officers (DLCO) were known), a bleak, Nissen-hutted place much beset by the 'dreaded haar', the autumnal mist which rolled inexorably in from the sea. Here a young dynamic commander pilot was attempting reasonably successfully to teach 'batting' as a serious aid to deck landing. Previously, any pilot not flying at the time was likely to be asked to have a go on the 'bats', a pair of large discs of framed yellow silk with wooden handles.

Swordfish I L2824 on the lift of HMS *Argus* during trials by the FRU during 1938 and 1939. (Fox Photos via *Aeroplane*)

A DCLO working hard to get this Swordfish back down safely on the deck.

Batting was not a popular occupation, combining the routine tedium of a ground job with the unforeseeable hazards of inexperienced pilots trying to deckland. It had one point in its favour; batsmen, after completing the course at East Haven usually went to sea. I somehow felt that the time had come in my life for prolonged exposure to duty-free.

The 'old biscuit tin'

My appointment was, agreeably enough, to the training carrier HMS *Argus*. After a short, hectic visit the previous year I would now be able to enjoy a spell in comfort as one of the ship's company. Unfortunately not for long because after 26 years of life it was going out of commission. As the autumn mists returned to the Clyde and clouds seldom uncovered the peaks of Arran, the 'old biscuit tin' prepared herself for a final, light flying programme.

Day begins with the pipe, "Range two Swordfish". The lift ascends, bell ringing, from the hangar, the aircraft have their wings spread and are pushed to the after end of the flight deck. Engines are run up, arrester wires raised and lowered to the hissing of compressed air, and the batting screen is raised. Finally *Argus* turns slowly into wind as the compass clicks round, the flags blow up and down the deck, the 'green' is flown in the Captain's starboard wing bridge, 'Wings' puts out the 'Affirmative' from the port bridge and with minimum fuss the Swordfish are flown off. Derek, the tall elegant batsman (not surprisingly, many years later to be an Admiral) strolls down the deck to his platform. Before the pupil pilots return a Swordfish comes in from Abbotsinch Air Station (HMS *Sanderling*). The pilot, Pat, is one of the 'clockwork mice' squadron, so-called because their thankless task is to deckland continuously to train batsmen; the CO has over 1,000 decklandings. This morning Pat says he's visiting *Argus* because he's exhausted his wine bill, not only back at Abbotsinch but also in *Ravager,* the other training carrier. "Bar's not open yet," says Wings. "Anyway, Pat, get the hell out of the way, we're working in this ship."

A Swordfish of 785 Squadron from Crail was lucky not to end up in the Firth of Forth after this landing on *Argus*.

"Most unusual," says Pat, "Fred Carno strikes camp," and he disappears down the bridge ladder. The flight deck party strikes down his aircraft before the two pupil pilots in their Swordfish are brought on effortlessly by Derek.

After lunch I called in at the hangar where Gillie, the Air Engineer Officer, was feverishly servicing one of the ancient Swordfish.

"Isn't it ready yet?"

"Of course, it's ready."

"OK I'll range it."

"Well, wait a tick..." Gillie was an RNVR Lt. with owlish spectacles and a facetious sense of humour. He spent most of the day on the Flying Bridge being funny about the flying programme. When un-serviceability threatened he retired resentfully into the hangar.

Back on deck I find the doc, a Surgeon Lt. Cdr. and 'Scratch', the Captain's secretary, have come up to 'goof'. Scratch inevitably reminds every one of the time during a crisis that he acted as FDO. On the inter-bridge telephone the jovial navigator draws our attention to a 'Wellington' as some stray Beaufighter passes overhead. In the Flying Bridge Pat is now arguing with 'Wings' about the possibility of shooting down seagulls with Verey cartridges. *Argus* settles down to the afternoon's flying.

Time to go in bat

After a week or so Derek let me do some batting. On the approach of the fourth Swordfish* I saw that the pupil pilot was too nose-down... I gave him an attitude signal... he's too high, bring him down... check that port drift... more engine, up, up... steady... attitude... Christ, he's going to drop out of the sky, engine... engine... ENGINE... WAVE HIM OFF. The words screamed in my head as I gave the pilot the circulating signal to go round again. The Swordfish made a staggering dive at the deck, port wing down... and as I jumped into the safety net I heard the roar of the accelerating engine... then a long, rending crash... an engine splutter... and silence. I picked myself out of the net, hands trembling and blood pounding. Hanging wretchedly over the side on an arrester wire, its nose trailing in the sea, its fabric torn and flapping, was the Swordfish. The pilot was beginning to clamber gingerly out of the cockpit.

"Wasn't your fault," said 'Wings', "he should have taken a wave-off. But don't leave it so late another time."

"Please God, let it be washed away," said Gillie, peering hopefully over the side at the dangling Swordfish.

"Captain will be livid if it means going back to Greenock tonight," said 'Wings'. A few minutes later the aircraft shifted slightly in the water, toppled clear of the slackened arrester wire and drifted astern, sinking. I continued batting until tea time without further incident. The Captain always finished flying at 1730 to enable him to be back at Rothesay in time for dinner. The Steering Position now emerged out of the flight deck, the White Ensign was transferred back from the quarter-deck and soon Special Sea Dutymen would close up on the fo'castle as we neared the anchorage. I had a shave, a bath, and put on a clean, white shirt. As I came to appreciate, this was the most pleasant time of day in harbour routine. The cares and grime of work were washed away, ahead lay an evening in well-found comfort of good food, very cheap drink and agreeable company. Stewards looked after one's things, made a note of what one drank, served at table; it wasn't a bad life for a twenty-one-year-old. I met Gillie at the entrance to the ante-room and we crossed to the bar.

"Two gins, please, Bridal."

"No ice this evening?"

"No, sir. Something's wrong with the machine." "Ah, me," said Gillie, "What we have to put up with in wartime."

Nocturnal training

Occasionally a course of Swordfish pilots arrived for night deck landings; this threw the ship into resentful activity. The deck lighting had to be uncovered, the night 'bats' sought from remote lockers and in the hangar Gillie huffily began fixing bulbs into rusty sockets and rewiring ancient aircraft. A cold bleak wind swept over the flight deck, the engines roared and stabbed the darkness with flame. On a fine clear night I found the wind and movement of the ship through the dark water quite exhilarating at first.

Whilst Derek did the batting I was responsible for marshalling and flying off the aircraft. I stood at the wing-tip as the pilot ran up the engine, the airframe bucking and straining with pent-up power against the chocks. When the pilot was ready he signalled with his thumb, I shone my green torch down the deck at the bridge; as soon as I got the answering green I raised my red and green

There was not a large margin for error on the deck of a moving aircraft carrier, but luckily for most pilots and crews under training, an accident in a Stringbag was usually survivable.

A Swordfish picks up the first of four arrestor cables across the deck of *Argus* in a perfect demonstration of how to land on a carrier.

torches at the pilot, waved away the chockmen from the wheels, raised my green torch, circling it slowly... the engine accelerated to the crescendo... I dipped the torch and the Swordfish roared away down the deck... I braced myself against the sudden buffet of hot air from the slipstream. As I climbed down into the catwalk Derek was beginning to adjust the cups of orange light which replaced the daytime 'bats'; from beyond the dazzle of the deck lighting I heard the clang of the uprising barrier.

The night grew colder, the engine roar and the slipstream began to weary mind and body, the flying programme went on and on as the loudspeaker at the batting platform crackled its repetitive orders; "Change pilots"... "re-fuel that aircraft"... "taxi that aircraft ahead of the barrier"... "range one Swordfish."

There was a twenty-minute break as *Argus* steamed downwind. I went below to the Pilots crewroom on the Operations flat. The pupil pilots were lounging in chairs, smoking and talking; empty cocoa cups littered the table and there was that weary staleness that marks crewrooms at night in the dim light of the blue bulbs. A time when one's mouth tastes of tiredness and people look at their watches and say, "Let's get started and finish the bloody thing." Derek came in, slightly dishevelled but wide awake and grinning; "You're doing OK, keep it up." I returned to the flight deck to find 'Wings' arguing with Gillie about bee-keeping. It seemed hours later when Derek said, "Last landing," and the ship piped "Hands secure flying stations."

More cocoa was served in the wardroom; the pilots, tired but cheerful, recalled incidents in the night's flying with amused relief. In my cabin bunk, as I reached for the light switch, heard the bubbling swish of the sea against the bulkhead and felt the air from the fan, I reflected thankfully that today would be a day of rest.

Relegated to deck-landing training during its latter service, *Argus* was earmarked for decommissioning on January 27, 1944 but remained in service for a further eight months. In March 1945, it was to be converted into an aircraft freighter but instead became an accommodation ship at Chatham until May 1946, when it was prepared for scrapping. By December, it was sold to be broken up at Inverkeithing, the final resting place of many Royal Navy ships.

An 'Act of Faith'

One of the few disadvantages of the easy routine which *Argus* followed that autumn was the Captain's insistence on a church service after Divisions each Sunday. Unlike other small carriers *Argus* possessed her own Royal Marines, therefore her own band; church service was a full-scale ritual in the hangar.

The chaplain was partly to blame for this. An evangelical young man who, two months before had been fluttering energetically about the parish of one of England's lesser known spas, brought his bright religious fervour unchanged to the needs of an RN church service. He seemed not to discriminate between his erstwhile congregation to whom church-going was a pleasure and his present one to whom it was a parade. The lengthy sermons which had indulged wealthy old ladies were agony to men whose main concern was catching the 1200 liberty boat.

As a concession to his present congregation on one occasion the chaplain attempted to portray Christianity in flying terms. It had been his one diverting sermon. Beginning with simple parallels he had involved himself in an increasing tangle of wild inaccuracies, much appreciated for once by his entire audience. One particular phrase went down well with the pilots: "Faith", he had said, "is your joystick." From then onwards 'Wings' unfailingly referred to a barrier crash as an Act of Faith. The end of church service in *Argus* was typical. After the order, "Fall out the officers," there was a single movement down the ante-room. On the bar, already lined up by the steward, were a dozen large gins.

But *Argus's* days were numbered; soon she would pay off and sail up Gare Loch, that sad limbo of old warships**. Before then I received a draft chit to HMS *Tracker,* an American-built escort carrier.

Farewell *Argus*

One windy October day I had a farewell drink in *Argus* as she lay at Tail o' the Bank, Greenock, and humped my luggage across by boat to my new ship. She had a gangway down on the port side and I made my soon familiar way up the clattering steps, saluted the officer-of-the-watch on the sponson, tripped over the Oerlikon mountings, pushed aside the curtains and entered the half-dark hangar, now empty of aircraft, and went down a deck to the wardroom.

The squadron was disembarked and I felt very much the new boy knowing none of the ship's officers. 'Wings', a small genial Lt. Cdr. RN ('Tich') with a very faded DSC ribbon introduced himself and bought me a gin. I felt if not exactly at home at least welcome. He told me about HMS *Tracker:* she and the squadron had been operating for almost a year, mostly on the convoy run to Gibraltar, with an occasional sortie into the Atlantic. This was to be their first Russian convoy, the so-called 'Kola run', named after the inlet near Murmansk.

We sailed on Saturday, October 14 from Greenock. It was a doubly inauspicious departure; because of Friday 13 sailing had been postponed a day and someone had dropped a cat overboard.

* This could have been one of two 'over the side' Swordfish incidents which took place on the *Argus* during July and August 1944. The first took place on July 22, involving Swordfish V4434/B flown by Sub Lt G Oldroyd, the second on August 23, involving Swordfish HS315/M flown by Sub Lt N F Lancaster.

** The very last take-off from the deck of HMS *Argus* took place on September 27, 1944

Chapter 11

'Lily'

'Boy's Own'

As a follow-on to operating aircraft from small decks, mention should be made about plans for a floating aerodrome with the code-name 'Lily'. The idea was not new: *Boy's Own* comics of the 1930s had envisaged such platforms in their stories and the idea had been discussed before in military circles. The advantages were obvious: it could be easily assembled/disassembled by relatively unskilled personnel and located in areas near the action, in fact being able to follow a moving front by being towed short distances. No one had come up with a workable plan, the main problem being how to compensate for undulating tidal waters.

The Royal Navy sponsored a floating aerodrome idea by a Mr R M Hamilton, a professional inventor who had served in the early part of the war as a Petty Officer in the Royal Naval Patrol Service. He had caught their Lordships' attention when he successfully designed a floating surface code-named 'Swiss Roll'. The idea was very basic and consisted of nothing note than a reinforced tarpaulin over some fencing strips which strengthened the surface tension of water. Hamilton had tested it himself by putting a section across a local stream and riding over it, first on a pedal cycle and then on a motorbike, including a passenger. It was used in conjunction with Mulberry Harbour sections following the D-Day landings on 6 June 1944.

A floating aerodrome

Eventually, with the help of a mathematical friend, J S Herbert, a housemaster at Eton College, Hamilton devised a floating aerodrome. It was constructed of 1,100 hexagonal-topped steel buoyancy chambers, the top of each chamber being 6ft (1.8m) in diameter and 3ft (0.9m) deep. By means of lugs on each of the six sides of the hexagon, each chamber was bolted to its neighbour, making a

'LILY', the Royal Navy's experimental floating airstrip in Lamlash harbour just after a high-speed launch has passed its length to demonstrate how well it copes with waves.

Lt Ray Jeffs prepares his Swordfish for another take off from the 'Lily' runway in the spring of 1945.

continuous structure on the honeycomb principle. The bolts were a loose fit so that the whole structure was completely flexible, undulating with the surface of the water. To increase stability, at each end were chambers that were 12ft (3.7m) deep. The structure was assembled with a working distance of 540 x 75ft (165 x 23m) wide. The complete landing strip could be moored in such a way that it swung with tide and wind, so that aircraft could take-off, approach and land into wind.

The strip was assembled on the surface of Lamlash harbour in the Isle of Arran. It was thought a Swordfish would provide an ideal testing machine (along with the Auster light spotter aircraft) and Lt Ray Jeffs was selected to carry out the trials. Lt Jeffs had been flying Swordfish from MAC-ships, which gave him the right background for the job, and he recalls the trials:

'Before we started these trials, I went over to Lamlash Harbour to have a look at 'Lily' so that I'd have a fair idea of what was going to happen when I was flying from the strip. I was amazed to see how flexible the strip was – each little wave was accurately reproduced, and it didn't seem possible that an aircraft of 9,000lb could operate safely. From the air, the strip looked quite solid and its usable size, 520 x 60ft, was in fact up to 100ft longer than the flight deck on MAC-ships. I'd served in these ships on the Atlantic convoy route for just over 18 months.

The strip, officials, observers and aircraft were all ready and I set off. I, for one, held my breath as I approached to land on. The main difference between landing on the strip and a carrier was that the approach was made so low over the water, the freeboard of the strip being only 17in high! The undulations could not be seen until the aircraft was quite close to the strip and even then they seem pretty small. In calm weather the landings and hooking of the arrestor wire were exactly the same as on a carrier, except of course, as the aircraft touched down there was a prolonged clanging from the cans. This could be heard above the engine noise. As the Swordfish came to rest its weight caused an indentation of about 10in.

Taking off was rather frightening at first – the effect of the groove caused by the aircraft's weight was like driving through deep sand when you are on the point of becoming bogged down. The Swordfish, which was fully loaded for its type, was fitted with rocket-assisted take-off gear and when this was fired the aircraft jumped forward and the groove got shallower as the aircraft speed picked up. The trials were most successful, with me landing on and flying off in winds down to 7kt. Here lies another advantage of the strip: on the carrier when we wanted to fly the skipper had to leave the convoy to steam into wind; with the strip buoyed it could swing so that you got the best wind down the runway.

'Lily' was constructed of over 1,000 hexagonal-topped steel buoyancy chambers; the only negative point from the pilot's point of view was the horrendous clanging noise they made when the aircraft was running along them.

A successful day of landing and taking off almost came to an abrupt end during one take-off when the tailwheel of Lt Jeffs' Swordfish picked up one of the arrestor wires. Here the fully loaded Swordfish struggles to gain speed with the offending wire trailing behind.

MAN-MADE ISLANDS AND FLOATING BRIDGES AND THE SCIENCE AND THE INVENTOR

One of many successful take-offs from 'Lily' with and without the RATOG mounted under the Swordfish III.

> **"It was in 1944 that the first practical result was employed, the 'Swiss Roll' pier, used in the Normandy invasion."**

British scientists have found a way of increasing the natural surface tension of water, making it technically possible to build a mid-Atlantic aerodrome or a floating cross-channel bridge, it was disclosed by the Admiralty in September 1945. This latest discovery in engineering-on-water began when an inventor's brain-wave sent him motor-cycling at 50mph along a tarpaulin stretched over a river ford. The new discovery has been sponsored and developed by the Royal Navy, and brings dramatic dreams within the realms of actuality.

Ordinary tension will support a needle on the water's surface. By putting a flexible synthetic surface on the sea, and by increasing the tension about 400,000 times, it has been found possible to support heavy lorries and aircraft in mid-ocean. One practical result of the discovery is the production of man-made 'islands', composed of hundreds of hexagonal buoyancy cans, 'islands' which can be built to any shape or length required, and which can be easily dismantled, transported and reassembled. Another, which has already stood up to the severe practical tests of war, is the 'Swiss roll', a floating pier that can be rolled up, carried on board a ship and later rolled out again from ship to shore. This pier is nearly 20 times as light as a Bailey bridge of equal length, yet it will carry a nine-ton lorry.

Inventor of these new devices is Mr. R. M. Hamilton, of Victoria Street, London, who served at the beginning of war as a Petty Officer in the Royal Naval Patrol Service. He is an inventor by profession. Co-operating on the involved mathematical calculations required was Mr J S Herbert, Housemaster at Eton College. "Further developments form the original discovery are being made", Mr Hamilton said, "but for a time their nature must remain secret".

It was in 1944 that the first practical result was employed, the 'Swiss Roll' pier, used in the Normandy invasion. In this flexible canvas-and-wood jetty, a tension of 18 to 30 tons is applied to any length stretching from ship to beach and the result is that a laden lorry can be driven ashore in safety over the sea. Some 2,700ft of 'Swiss Roll' were in continual use at the invasion harbour at Arromanches in spite of the appalling weather that, unluckily, was encountered there.

The Navy's latest experiments, only recently concluded, have been with a further development of the same fundamental principle, the 'Lily' floating airstrip. Given its name because of its resemblance to a carpet of lily leaves on a pond, 'Lily' is a very different proposition to 'Swiss Roll'. It consists of numbers of buoyancy cans with hexagonal surfaces, so linked together that they 'give' in a controlled manner to the motion of the sea from any direction, yet remain sufficiently rigid to take the weight of a heavy aircraft. Whereas in 'Swiss Roll' tension is applied externally, 'Lily's' hexagonal surfaces, when linked together, create their own tension.

The dream of Atlantic aerodromes has hitherto been unattainable because it has not been possible to build large enough storm-proof flat-surface structures. Modern transport aircraft would need a carrier or a strip twice the length of the *Queen Elizabeth*, largest ship in the world. Such a floating structure has hitherto been impractical. The Navy's new 'seadrome' can be transported in ships and assembled anywhere. With the present size buoyancy can, a 'Lily' 2,500ft long, could be transported in three merchant ships.

'Lily's' possibilities for bridge-building are underlined by those responsible for its development. "To mention a cross-Channel bridge immediately places you with straws in your hair", said Mr Herbert, the mathematician, "but we can say that it would be possible to build a floating bridge 22 miles long that would not break up in a sea."

Only on one occasion did we nearly meet with disaster, and that was actually the last take-off that day. I was sure that both the aircraft and I were in for a ducking. There I was (as they say in the RAF) with engine and rockets doing their utmost to get me airborne and the wire trying to hold me back. All was well, I managed to pull the aircraft up, although I wished I had a pair of sculls at the time.'

One of the observers was Lt May and he says: 'The plane revved up and moved off, very slowly at first, pushing a wave in front of it with a smaller wave coming up astern, as with a motor-boat. But I watched in horror as the Swordfish's tailwheel caught on a wire halfway along the runway, but the plane carried on and only just cleared the mooring buoy at the end of the strip. Then it skimmed the water, hanging on to its propeller, trying not to slip back, but it made it and climbed away.'

Chapter 12

The Royal Navy Historic Flight (RNHF) and the Swordfish

The RNHF

Formed at RNAS Yeovilton in 1972, the RNHF was created specifically to operate an increasing number of historic aircraft being donated to the Royal Navy.

An early arrival in 1960 was Swordfish II, LS326 (donated by Westland Aircraft), which had been maintained in airworthy condition by Fairey at White Waltham since its purchase from storage at Worthy Down soon after the end Second World War.

Venerable Swordfish II LS326, of the RNHF, which first entered FAA service in August 1943. This popular airshow performer has received a great deal of attention in recent years, which will hopefully see the aircraft remain airworthy long time to come. (Via Martyn Chorlton)

Hawker Siddeley donated the first of three Sea Furies destined to be operated by the flight in 1971. Firefly AS.5, WB271 followed in 1972. Both of these aircraft have been lost in accidents: Sea Fury FB.11, TF956 in June 1989 and the Firefly at Duxford in July 2003. Despite these setbacks, the flight has grown from strength to strength and today it operates two Swordfish, one Sea Fury, the world's only airworthy Seahawk, and a Chipmunk for crew training and tailwheel experience.

The Swordfish – LS326

The longest serving of the two Swordfish that are now part of the RNHF is Blackburn-built LS326, which was first delivered to the FAA on August 17, 1943 from Sherburn-in-Elmet. After serving at Donibristle and Machrihanish, the aircraft joined 836 Squadron, to serve aboard the Mac-ship MV *Rapana* as part of 'L' Flight with the code 'L2'. The *Rapana* helped to protect the North Atlantic convoys, the ship and its aircraft travelling from Maydown (the main operating airfield for 836 Squadron) and occasionally Machrihanish, to Dartmouth, Nova Scotia, and back.

During this period of LS326's service, the aircraft was involved in one incident on November 28, 1943 when a heavy landing on the *Rapana* broke an axle fork securing pin and the lower main spar – the latter by a heavy handed deck party.

In February 1944, LS326 was allocated to 'K' Flight, which had only been formed the previous December aboard the Mac-ship MV *Empire MacCullum*. From early April 1944,

Possibly one of the earliest images of LS326, pictured taxying at North Weald on April 27, 1947. (via Martyn Chorlton)

LS326 has been a popular sight of airshows across the country since the early 1960s. The Swordfish is pictured at the SBAC Farnborough in 1964. (via Martyn Chorlton)

Empire MacCullum took on 'R' Flight and later 'T' Flight, while 'K' Flight appears to have been transferred to the MV *Empire MacDermott*, although this ship has never been credited to LS326's history before. It can be confirmed that LS326 was back on dry land at Maydown in early November (more likely late October) and on November 19 it was transferred to Belfast (Sydenham aka HMS *Gadwall*). From here the war began to quieten down for the Swordfish, which was moved again to the RDU (Receipt & Despatch Unit) Culham and RDU Worthy Down; the latter presumably occurred circa 1945.

While hundreds of other Swordfish were now being scrapped, LS326 seems to have been overlooked but did not escape the attention of the Fairey Aircraft Company. In early 1947 the aircraft was purchased from the Royal Navy, evidently in airworthy condition, as it was put into immediate use as a display aircraft at various RAeS Garden parties across the country. The earliest known party attended by LS326 took place at North Weald on April 27, which was also where the oldest known image (to date) of this famous aircraft was captured.

By 1948, LS326 was placed in storage at White Waltham, where the aircraft was not held in the highest esteem by the workforce and soon started looking worse for wear. Luckily, Sir Richard Fairey stepped in and arranged for the Swordfish to be rebuilt back to its former glory. The aircraft was not fully restored until October 1955, by which time it had been placed on the civilian register as G-AJVH, which it never displayed – the Swordfish retaining its true identity as LS326. Operated from White Waltham, the aircraft was finished in a Fairey blue and silver colour scheme.

LS326 made an appearance at Lee-on-Solent in June 1959, where it was seen wearing the fictitious code '5A' which it would continue to display into the late 1980s. This sighting at Lee was probably recorded during the filming of the classic war film 'Sink the Bismarck', which was released in February 1960.

1960 also saw Fairey swallowed up by Westlands, who had no interest in maintaining a wartime Swordfish, but did recognise its worth, by donating it to the Royal Navy in October. For many years the Royal Navy flew LS326 in its 'on screen' *Bismarck* colours but in 1984, in celebration of the 40th Anniversary of the Normandy landings, the Swordfish had a set of invasion stripes added. From 1987 its original appearance as part of 'L' Flight of 836 Squadron was re-instated, including the code 'L2' on its fuselage.

Adopted by the City of Liverpool in May 1996, the aircraft later underwent a thorough rebuild at BAe Systems Brough which saw this popular performer away from the airshow circuit for nine years. Back in the air on July 1, 2008, LS326 continues to please the crowds across the country today.

W5856

The second of the RNHF's Swordfish is another 'Blackfish', built from a batch of 100 aircraft under Contract B31192/39 in 1941. Swordfish I, W5856 was delivered to 82 MU (Aircraft Packing Depot) at Lichfield on October 21, 1941, where the aircraft was consigned to a crate on November 15, for despatch to Gibraltar on board the SS *Empire Morn*.

The aircraft's history from its delivery to Gibraltar is a little sketchy but it is presumed the Swordfish served with the Mediterranean Fleet before it was returned to Fairey at Stockport for refurbishment in December 1942. By February 1943, the aircraft was ready to return to FAA service but instead jumped

Being waved at by anyone in an aircraft would always put a smile on the face of a young lad at an airshow; the crew of the Swordfish were always expert at it! (via Martyn Chorlton)

LS326 pictured in pristine condition at the Goodwood Revival on September 18, 2011.

Fully restored in the colours and codes of 810 Squadron, Swordfish I W5856 is pictured at Brough on May 22, 1993. (via Martyn Chorlton)

ship to join the RAF and 9 (P)AFU (21 Group) at Errol located on the northern bank of the River Tay, on April 14, 1943. The (P)AFU ranged far and wide across the region and W5856 would also have operated from Findo Gask.

In February 1944, W5856 was loaned to RAF Manston for 'tactical trials' for a short period but was back at Errol by early March. The aircraft's return to 9 (P)AFU was a short lived one because on March 5, the Pegasus engine failed on take-off, causing W5856 to stall onto a road and crash through a fence. The damage was not serious but the aircraft was shipped by road to 76 MU at Wroughton, its RAF days now over.

By July 1944 the Swordfish was once more ready for the air, but this time was flown to Hamble and then Eastleigh, where it was prepared for service overseas again, although this time in Canada. W5856 was prepared for transit on July 18 and on October 15, 1944 was on the books of 1 NAGS at RCAF Yarmouth but was not officially TOS (Taken on strength) by the RCAF until December 15, 1944. RCAF service was short though, as W5856 was in storage at RCAF Mount Hope from April 1945 and SOC on August 21, 1946 with 536.15hrs of flying time under its belt.

Along with many other ex-RCAF Swordfish, W5856 was sold on the civilian market in the early 1950s. First owner was Ernie Simmonds from Ontario who passed the aircraft on to a farmer by the name of J F Carter, who used the aircraft for crop dusting at his farm near Monroeville, Alabama. It is not clear how long the aircraft was used in this role, but by the time Sir William Roberts, owner of Strathallan Collection discovered the Swordfish, it was in a pretty sorry but complete state. W5856 then re-crossed Atlantic for the first time in over 30 years, this time in crates to Strathallan, arriving on August 7, 1977.

It is not known how much restoration work was carried out by the collection, which was closed to the general public in the late 1980s, but by 1990 W5856 was purchased by British Aerospace for the Swordfish Heritage Trust (now Fly Navy Heritage Trust). The meticulous restoration of the Swordfish continued at Brough, while the Pegasus engine was completely rebuilt by Rolls Royce at Filton. The completed aircraft was first seen by the general public at Brough on May 22, 1993. Resplendent in the pre-war markings of 810 Squadron, with codes 'A2A' the Swordfish I has been operated by the RNHF ever since.

Right: While the flight instruments of the Swordfish are generally were they should be, all the supporting levers, cocks and switches can only be described as 'haphazard'! (via Martyn Chorlton)

Below: Very early photo of Swordfish III NF389 at White Waltham on May 6, 1951; the aircraft was still on the strength of the ATDU at the time. (via Martyn Chorlton)

Swordfish I W5856 pictured over the Needles, Isle of Wight. (BAe Systems via Martyn Chorlton)

W
A2A W5856

NF389 warms its Pegasus engine through before carrying out another sortie for the ATDU. (*Aeroplane*)

Aircraft of the RNHF from 1972 to date					
Aircraft	**Serial**	**To RNHF**	**Fate**		**Current status**
Swordfish I	W5856	1993			Airworthy
Swordfish II	LS326	1960			Airworthy
Swordfish III	NF389	1994			Static
Firefly AS.5	WB271	Sep 1972	Lost Jul 12, 2003		
Sea Fury FB.11	TF956	Jan 21, 1972	Lost Jun 10, 1989		
Sea Fury T.20	WG655	Jun 29, 1976	Lost Jul 14, 1990		
Sea Fury FB.11	VR930	Feb 1, 1990			Airworthy
Sea Hawk FGA.6	WV908	Sep 28, 1982			Airworthy
Chipmunk T.10	WK608	Jul 23, 1993			Airworthy

NF389 – waiting in the wings

A third Swordfish, which has been instrumental in keeping LS326 and W5856 in the air over the years, is Mk III, NF389.

First delivered on April 15, 1944, the aircraft languished in storage before being transferred to the RAF on March 13, 1945. Not credited with serving with any RAF unit, the aircraft was later delivered to 29 MU at High Ercall on August 29, 1946, in preparation for transfer back to the FAA. This duly took place on September 19, 1946 when the aircraft was delivered to Donibristle the Arbroath from where it joined to the ATDU at Gosport for torpedo trials on September 13, 1948. After major servicing at Hamble from November 1950, the Swordfish re-joined the ATDU (which later moved to Culdrose on May 9, 1951) for further torpedo trial work.

NF389's service with ATDU came to an end on August 23, 1952 when it force landed at St Merryn. By March the following year the Swordfish still had a role to play in the FAA because it was 'on nominal charge' to 781 Squadron (a unit that originally flew the Swordfish between September 1940 and February 1943) for show purposes.

Like LS326, NF389 was used during the filming of 'Sink the Bismarck' and is also believed to have made a few cameos in several other un-named films during the 1950s. By the early 1960s the aircraft displayed the code '5B' and was placed on static display at RNAS Lee-on-Solent. It was while at Lee that components were slowly removed in order to keep LS326 in the air until, over 20 years later, the aircraft was sent to Brough for static restoration. During this process during the early 1990s the aircraft was also used as a pattern to help rebuild W5856.

In the summer of 1994 the aircraft was associated directly with the RNHF for the first time, the Swordfish being moved down from Brough for a static display outside the flight's hangar at Yeovilton for the station air day in July. Following this brief public appearance, NF389 was placed in storage and once again was used as a 'hangar queen' to keep LS326 and W5856 in the air. However, BAe offered to restore NF389 back to airworthy condition and on January 25, 1999, the Swordfish was back at Brough for a much deeper restoration programme, which was planned to take two years.

By now, NF389 had been christened 'City of Bristol' and was back down at Yeovilton with the promise of three airworthy Swordfish on the display circuit. However, it is believed that the aircraft is once again back in storage at Yeovilton and, at present, it will be doubtful of NF389 is ever seen back in the again.

Chapter 13

'Stringbag' Survivors

DK791

First delivered by Blackburn on November 11, 1941, our first survivor later joined 813 Squadron and was coded '4C'. The Swordfish, an Mk II, had a short career which came to an abrupt end on July 4, 1942 when the engine failed after take-off at North Front and the aircraft was ditched in the water, just over the sea wall.

It is not clear when the wreckage was recovered, but by 1986 the remains of DK791 are claimed to be in the hands of the Museum of Transport and Technology (MOTAT) in Auckland New Zealand. It is also not clear how much of the original DK791, if anything, was used to create the replica aircraft which is serialled as DK791.

HS469

Swordfish II, HS469 was delivered to the FAA on February 10, 1943 followed by brief service with 841 Squadron at Manston. By late summer of 1943 the aircraft was crossing the Atlantic to Canada and was

The only example of what a 119 Squadron Swordfish III, complete with ASV would have looked like, is the pristinely restored NF370 located at the IWM, Duxford. (Martyn Chorlton)

TOS by the RCAF on September 2, 1943. Re-erected at Dartmouth, the aircraft joined 745 Squadron on August 28, 1943. Further service followed with 1 Wireless School at Mount Hope before the aircraft was SOC on August 17, 1946, with just 267.35hrs on the airframe.

Purchased by Mr Simmonds of Ontario, the aircraft languished in poor condition until the 1980s when it was recovered by a group of enthusiasts in the 1980s. 13 years later the aircraft was restored to airworthy condition in 1994 and donated to the Shearwater Aviation Museum, where it remains today.

HS491

Used to help restore HS469 and HS554, Swordfish Mk II, HS491 was first delivered by Blackburn on February 18, 1943 and was earmarked for RCAF service. The aircraft served with 745 Squadron RT Flt from October 1943 to December 1944 and then with 1 Wireless School. SOC from RCAF on August 2, 1946 the aircraft had only flown 155.05hrs.

The aircraft was later acquired by the National Aviation Museum of Canada, but since 2004, is undergoing restoration to static condition at Ta Qali Aircraft Museum in Malta.

HS498

Another Swordfish II, destined for RCAF service was HS498 which was delivered on February 20, 1943 and was TOS by the RCAF on April 22, 1943. The aircraft served with 745 Squadron RT Flt from September 1943 to November 1944 during which time it was converted to an Mk IV. A spell with 1 Wireless School followed before the aircraft was SOC on August 21, 1946.

The aircraft was later sold to Karl Enholder of Vancouver but today resides, in readiness for restoration at the Reynolds-Alberta Museum, Wetaskiwin, Alberta.

HS503

TOS by the RCAF on April 22, 1943, Swordfish II, HS503, joined 745 Squadron as 'J2' in June 1943. Following conversion to Mk IV and TT standard the aircraft served with 754 Squadron between June 1944 and February 1945. SOC on August 21, 1945, the aircraft was one of several purchased by Mr Simmonds of Ontario, but this one found itself back in Britain many years later. On the strength of the RAF Museum at Cosford, the aircraft is currently out of the public eye at Stafford, in the reserve collection.

HS509

Swordfish II, HS509 was TOS by the RCAF on July 8, 1943 and served with 745 Squadron from August 1943 to March 1945, during which time it was converted to an Mk IV. SOC on September 4, 1946, parts from this aircraft were later used to restore HS469 and HS554. The aircraft is currently being stored at the National Aviation Museum of Canada.

HS554

Swordfish II, HS554 (C-GEVS) remains the only airworthy example in private hands, and will remain so for the foreseeable future.

The aircraft joined the RCAF on September 16, 1943 to serve with 745 Squadron RT Flt as 'U3' from November 1943 to February 1944. SOC on August 2, 1946, the aircraft was another Simmonds purchase which was later one of three acquired by Bob Spence of Muirkirk, Ontario.

First post-restoration flight was carried out on August 17, 1992. The aircraft is a regular and very popular participant at air shows in the southern Ontario area.

HS618

Delivered to the FAA on April 30, 1943, Swordfish II, HS618 served with 843 Squadron, 'C' from May. The aircraft was later damaged in a gale on board HMS *Hunter* in August 1943 and was relegated as a GI, A2001. The aircraft was later transferred to the RNEC at Manadon in 1960 but only a few years later was donated to the FAA Museum, where it remains today.

NF370

A very well-known example of a Swordfish III is NF370 at Duxford, an aircraft with very little history to its name. First delivered from Sherburn on April 1, 1944, the aircraft was on RAF charge from February 1945. The aircraft resided at Stretton from December 1946 to April 1950 and then onto Gosport from where it was acquired by the IWM and transported to Lambeth. Painted in colours to represent a 119 Squadron machine, the aircraft has been at Duxford since 1986.

NS122

The second airworthy Swordfish that can be found in a Canadian Museum is a Swordfish III which claims to be NS122. This aircraft was another from the Simmonds collection which deteriorated to such a degree, a definite identification was impossible.

The aircraft was purchased by the Canadian War Museum in September 1965 and today is on display at the Canada Aviation and Space Museum at Rockcliffe, Ottawa.

Unknown serials

One unknown Swordfish II is located at the National Air and Space Museum, Washington, and another Mk II, which was acquired in 1995, is undergoing restoration at the Aero Space Museum of Calgary. An ex-RCAF Mk II is also located at the Bristol Heritage Collection, Nashville, where it is hoped the aircraft will be returned to the air.

The bulk purchase of numerous ex-RCAF Swordfish during the late 1940s by Ernie Simmonds of Ontario, despite the condition they ended up in, certainly helped to save a large number of these aircraft for preservation today. Some of the Swordfish are pictured during a public auction in 1965. (via David H. Smith)

Spuriously serialled NS122, the restoration back to airworthy condition of this Swordfish III was nevertheless an outstanding achievement and it is a shame the aircraft is now museum-bound at the Canada Aviation and Space Museum. (via David H. Smith)

Chapter 14

Swordfish in Service

FAA Front-Line Swordfish Squadrons

810 Squadron	
(Ut fulmina de caelo (Like a thunderbolt from heaven)) *Aircraft*	
Swordfish I	Sep 1937-Mar 1943
Swordfish II	Mar 1942-Mar 1943
*Commanding Officers**	
Sqn Ldr H M Mellor MVO, RN	May 5, 1936
Capt N R M Skene, RM	Dec 9, 1938
Capt A C Newsom, RN	Jun 16, 1940
Lt Cdr M Johnstone, DSC, RN	Jul 16, 1940
Lt J V Hartley,	Sep 11, 1941
Lt Cdr R N Everett, RN	Dec 29, 1941
Lt Cdr W E Waters, RN	Jan 31, 1943
Lt Cdr (A) A J B Forde, RN	Mar 18, 1943

Stations/Ships
Gosport, Evanton, HMS *Courageous*, Southampton, Roborough, Old Sarum, HMS *Ark Royal*, Dekheila, Aboukir, Lee-on-Solent, Warmwell, Hatston, Wingfield, Arbroath, North Front, HMS *Furious*, Palisadoes, HMS *Illustrious*, Norfolk, HMS *Formidable*, High Ercall, Campbeltown, Machrihanish, Stamford Hill, Port Reitz, Kilindini, Tanga and Stretton
*Only COs listed during periods of service with the Swordfish

811 Squadron	
Aircraft	
Swordfish I	Oct 1936-Sep 1939
Swordfish II	Nov 1941-Dec 1944
Swordfish III	Jul 1944-Dec 1944
Commanding Officers	
Cdr RR Graham, RN	Sep 23, 1935
Lt Cdr L I G Richardson, RN	Feb 27, 1936
Sqn Ldr J A S Brown	Dec 12, 1937

811 Squadron		
Lt Cdr E O F Price, RN	Jan 21, 1938	
Unit disbanded	May 24, 1938	
Lt Cdr E O F Price, RN	May 24, 1938	
Lt Cdr S Borrett, RN	Jul 1, 1939	
Unit disbanded	Sep 17, 1939	
Lt Cdr W J Lucas, RN	Oct 29, 1941	
Lt Cdr H S Hayes, DSC, RN	Feb 27, 1942	
Lt J G Baldwin, RN	Jan 28, 1943	
Lt A S Kennard, DSC, RN	Apr 12, 1943	
Lt Cdr E B Morgan, RANVR	Nov 29, 1943	
Lt Cdr (A) E E G Emsley	Jul 27, 1944	
Unit disbanded	Dec 9, 1944	

Stations/Ships
Donibristle, HMS *Furious*, Gosport, Aboukir, Evanton, Lee-on-Solent, HMS *Courageous*, Arbroath, Machrihanish, Bircham Newton, Thorney Island, Hatston, HMS *Biter*, Ballykelly, Belfast, Inskip, North Front, Limavady, HMS *Vindex*, Crail, Stretton and Eglinton

812 Squadron		
(Dex aie (God aid)) *Aircraft*		
Swordfish I/SP	Dec 1936-Dec 1942	
Swordfish II	Oct 1942-Dec 1942	
Commanding Officers		
Lt Cdr C A N Hooper, RN	Nov 11, 1936	
Sqn Ldr N A P Pritchett, RAF	Nov 23, 1936	
Sqn Ldr J H Hutchinson, RAF	Apr 26, 1937	
Lt Cdr J D C Little, RN	Nov 1, 1938	
Lt Cdr A S Bolt, RN	Jun 16, 1939	
Lt Cdr W E Waters, DFC, RN	Sep 6, 1940	
Lt Cdr G A L Woods, RN	Nov 16, 1941	
Lt Cdr B J Prendergast, RN	May 30, 1942	
Unit disbanded	Dec 18, 1942	

Stations/Ships
HMS *Glorious*, Hal Far, Gosport, HMS *Courageous*, HMS *Malaya*, Dekheila, Manston, Prestwick, Ford, North Coates, Bircham Newton, Ford, Detling, St Eval, Crail, Topcliffe, Campbeltown, HMS *Argus*, Hatston, Twatt, HMS *Furious*, North Front, HMS *Ark Royal*, USS Wasp, Machrihanish, Lee-on-Solent and Docking

813 Squadron

(Full sails) Aircraft	
Swordfish I	Jul 1937-Mar 1943
Swordfish II	Nov 1942-Sep 1943
	Nov 1943-Jul 1944
Swordfish III	Jun 1944-May 1945
Commanding Officers	
Lt Cdr C R V Pugh, RN	Jan 18, 1937
Lt Cdr N Kennedy, DSC, RN	Sep 1, 1938
Lt Cdr D H Elles, RN	Jan 9, 1941
Lt Cdr A V Lyle, RN	Nov 25, 1941
Lt Cdr C Hutchinson, RN	Mar 25, 1942
Lt J H Ree, RN	Jun 27, 1943
Lt Cdr D A P Weatherall, RN	Aug 1, 1943
Unit disbanded	Oct 18, 1943
Lt Cdr (A) J R Parish DSC, RNVR	Nov 1, 1943
Lt Cdr (A) C A Allen, RNVR	Sep 2, 1944
Lt Cdr (A) S G Cooke, RNVR	Oct 12, 1944
Unit disbanded	May 15, 1945

Stations/Ships
Gosport, HMS *Eagle*, Hal Far, Seletar, Kai Tak, Wei-Hai-Wei, Penang, Kallang, Sembawang, Dekheila, HMS *Illustrious*, Maaten Ragush, Fuka, Port Sudan, Machrihanish, Lee-on-Solent, North Front, Tafaroui, Blida, Bone, HMS *Hunter*, Donibristle, Dunino, Inskip, Burscough, Maydown, HMS *Campania*, Abbotsinch, Hatston and HMS *Vindex*

814 Squadron

(In hoc signo vinces (In this sign you will conquer)) Aircraft	
Swordfish I	Dec 1938-Dec 1942
Commanding Officers	
Lt Cdr N S Luard, DSC	Dec 1, 1938
Mjr W H N Martin, RM	Dec 27, 1940
Lt A F Paterson, RN	Sep 25, 1942
Unit disbanded	Dec 31, 1942

Stations/Ships
Southampton, HMS *Ark Royal*, Warmwell, Worthy Down, Roborough, HMS *Hermes*, Hastings, Ouakam, Young's Field, Wellington, Wynberg, Stamford Hill, China Bay, Shaibah, Ratmalana, Port Reitz, Kokkolei, Colombo Racecourse and Katukurunda

815 Squadron	
(Strike deep) *Aircraft*	
Swordfish I	Oct 1939-Nov 1939
	Nov 1939-Feb 1943
Swordfish II	Mar 1943-Jul 1943
Commanding Officers	
Lt Cdr S Borrett, RN	Oct 9, 1939
Unit disbanded	Nov 10, 1939
Lt Cdr S Borrett, RN	Nov 23, 1939
Lt Cdr R A Kilroy, DFC, RN	Apr 17, 1940
Lt Cdr K Williamson, RN	Aug 3, 1940
Lt Cdr J de F Jago, RN	Nov 16, 1940
Lt Cdr F M A Torrens-Spence, RN	Mar 15, 1941
Lt Cdr T P Coode, RN	Oct 27, 1941
Lt Cdr P D Gick, RN	Dec 14, 1941
Lt Cdr (A) J W G Wellham, DSC, RN	Sep 29, 1942
Unit disbanded	Jul 24, 1943

Stations/Ships

Worthy Down, Cardiff, Bircham Newton, Ford, Detling, HMS *Illustrious*, Roborough, Campbeltown, Aboukir, Dekhelia, Fuka, Heraklion, Hal Far, Monastir, Maleme, Eleusis, Paramythia, Nicosia, Lakatamia, Maaten Bagush (LG.75), St Jean D'Acre, Amriya (LG.86), Sidi Barrani (LG.121), Gamil, Gaza, Mersah Matruh (LG.08), LG.139, Berka, El Magrun, Misurata, Ta Kali and Fayid

816 Squadron	
(Imitate the action of the tiger) *Aircraft*	
Swordfish I	Oct 1939-Nov 1941
	Feb 1942-Oct 1942
Swordfish II	Jun 1942-Mar 1943
	Apr 1943-Aug 1944
Commanding Officers	
Lt J Dalyell-Stead, RN (temp)	Oct 13, 1939
Lt Cdr H H Gardener, RN	Oct 19, 1939
Lt Cdr T G C Jameson, RN	May 6, 1940
Unit disbanded	Nov 13, 1941
Capt O Patch, RM	Feb 1, 1942
Lt R C B Stallard-Penoyre, RN	Oct 15, 1942
Lt P F Pryor, RN	Apr 22, 1943

816 Squadron		
Lt Cdr (A) F C Nottingham, DSC, RNVR	Jul 12, 1943	
Lt Cdr P Snow, RN	May 3, 1944	
Unit disbanded	Aug 1, 1944	

Stations/Ships

HMS *Furious*, HMS *Ark Royal*, Hatston, Abbotsinch, Campbeltown, Donibristle, Ternhill, Ford, Jersey, Prestwick, Bircham Newton, Evanton, North Coates, Detling, St Eval, Thorney Island, Eastleigh, Palisadoes, Norfolk, HMS *Avenger*, Lee-on-Solent, Machrihanish, HMS *Dasher*, Exeter, Fearn, Maydown, HMS *Tracker*, Argenta Field, HMS *Chaser*, Renfrew, Crail, Perranporth and St Merryn

818 Squadron		
(Sine mora (Without delay)) *Aircraft*		
Swordfish I	Aug 1939-Nov 1941	
Swordfish II	Oct 1942-Oct 1944	
Commanding Officers		
Lt Cdr J E Fenton, RN	Aug 30, 1939	
Lt Cdr P G O Sydney-Turner, RN	Mar 19, 1940	
Lt Cdr T P Coode, RN	Oct 24, 1940	
Lt Cdr T W B Shaw, DSC, RN	Jul 28, 1941	
Unit disbanded	Jun 24, 1942	
Lt Cdr A H Abrams, DSC, RN	Oct 22, 1942	
Lt Cdr (A) W H Lloyd, RNVR	Jul 7, 1943	
Unit disbanded	Oct 14, 1944	

Stations/Ships

Evanton, HMS *Ark Royal*, Hatston, Abbotsinch, HMS *Furious*, Campbeltown, Sealand, Ford, Thorney Island, Carew Cheriton, Aldergrove, North Front, Arbroath, Twatt, Machrihanish, HMS *Argus*, HMS *Formidable*, Juhu, Ratmalana, Katukurunda, Lee-on-Solent, Kirkistown, HMS *Unicorn*, Belfast, China Bay, Juhu, HMS *Atherling*, Wingfield and Cochin

819 Squadron		
(Redem feri claudum (Strike the foot that limps)) *Aircraft*		
Swordfish I	Jan 1940-Jan 1941	
	Oct 1941-Jun 1943	
Swordfish II	Apr 1942-Mar 1945	
Swordfish III	Aug 1944-Mar 1945	
Commanding Officers		

819 Squadron

Lt Cdr J W Hale, DSO, RN	Feb 12, 1940
Unit disbanded	Jan 14, 1941
Lt Cdr D G Goodwin, DSC, RN	Oct 25, 1941
Lt H S Mc N Davenport, RN	Apr 10, 1942
Lt (A) O A G Oxley, RN	Jan 23, 1943
Lt Cdr (A) P D T Stevens, RNVR	Apr 20, 1944
Unit disbanded	Mar 10, 1945

Stations/Ships
Ford, West Freugh, Detling, Roborough, HMS *Illustrious*, Bermuda, Abbotsinch, Dekheila, Fuka, Heraklion, Hal Far, Lee-on-Solent, Crail, Twatt, Hatston, Donibristle, Machrihanish, HMS *Avenger*, Langham, Bircham Newton, Thorney Island, Fearn, HMS *Archer*, Ballykelly, Belfast, Kaldadarnes, St Merryn, Maydown, Ayr, Eglinton, HMS *Activity*, Inskip, Limavady, Swingfield, Biggin Hill, St Croix (B.63), Maldeghem (B.65) and Knocke-le-Zoute (B.83)

820 Squadron

(Tutamen et ultor (Safeguard and avenger))	
Aircraft	
Swordfish I	Sep 1937-Jun 1941
Commanding Officers	
Lt Cdr A C G Ermen, RN	Aug 19, 1937
Lt Cdr G B Hodgkinson, RN	Jan 7, 1939
Lt Cdr A Yeoman, RN	Aug 29, 1940
Lt Cdr J A Stewart-Moore, RN	Oct 27, 1940

Stations/Ships
HMS *Courageous*, Evanton, Eastleigh, Southampton, HMS *Ark Royal*, Hal Far, Lee-on-Solent, Gosport, Ford, Donibristle, Ford, Dekheila, Hatston, Campbeltown and North Front

821 Squadron

(À coup sûr (With a sure or certain blow))	
Aircraft	
Swordfish I	Sep 1937-Jan 1941
	Jul 1941-Mar 1942
Commanding Officers	
Lt Cdr G R M Clifford	Sep 21, 1936
Lt Cdr J A D Wroughton, RN	Mar 29, 1939
Lt Cdr G M Duncan, RN	May 24, 1939
Lt Cdr J A D Wroughton, RN	Sep 14, 1939
Mjr W H N Martin, RM	May 29, 1940

821 Squadron		
Lt Cdr R R Wood, RN	Dec 27, 1940	
Unit disbanded	Jan 21, 1941	
Lt Cdr C W B Smith	Jul 15, 1941	
Mjr A C Newsom, RM	Mar 12, 1942	

Stations/Ships
Evanton, Gosport, Lee-on-Solent, Southampton, Portland, HMS *Courageous*, Eastchurch, HMS *Ark Royal*, Hatston, Ouakam, Ford, Dekhelia, Donibristle, Prestwick, HMS *Argus*, North Front, Hal Far, Candia, Detling, Twatt, Machrihanish, Sumburgh and Arbroath

822 Squadron		
Aircraft		
Swordfish I	Aug 1937-May 1939	
	May 1939-Sep 1939	
Swordfish II	Oct 1941-Mar 1942	
Commanding Officers		
Lt Cdr A M Rundle, RN	Mar 14, 1936	
Lt Cdr J B Buckley, RN	Apr 21, 1938	
Lt Cdr K Williamson, RN	Jul 28, 1938	
Unit disbanded	May 24, 1939	
Lt Cdr W H G Saunt, RN	May 25, 1939	
Lt Cdr H L McCulloch, RN	Jun 1, 1939	
Lt Cdr P W Humphreys, RN	Jul 1, 1939	
Unit disbanded	Sep 17, 1939	
Mjr A R Burch, DSC, RM	Oct 15, 1941	

Stations/Ships
Gosport, HMS *Furious*, Evanton, Manston, Donibristle, HMS *Courageous*, Southampton, Lee-on-Solent, Gosport, Millom and Hatston

823 Squadron		
(Vigueur de dessus (Strength from above))		
Aircraft		
Swordfish I	Nov 1936-Dec 1940	
	Nov 1941-Apr 1942	
Commanding Officers		
Lt Cdr G C Dickens, RN	Aug 30, 1935	
Lt Cdr D W MacKendrick, RN	May 21, 1937	
Lt Cdr R A Kilroy, RN	Feb 1, 1938	
Lt Cdr R D Watkins, RN	May 24, 1939	
Lt Cdr C J T Stephens, RN	May 27, 1940	
Lt Cdr D H Elles, RN	Jul 3, 1940	

823 Squadron

Lt Cdr (A) A J D Harding, DSC, RN	Nov 1, 1941	

Stations/Ships
Hal Far, HMS *Glorious*, Gosport, Aboukir, Dekhelia, Hatston, Evanton, Crail, Fraserburgh, Machrihanish and Lee-on-Solent

824 Squadron

(Spectat ubique spiritus (The wind everywhere looks on))
Aircraft

Swordfish I	Apr 1937-Aug 1942
	Oct 1942-Jan 1943
Swordfish II	Nov 1942-Oct 1944

Commanding Officers

Sqn Ldr A B Woodhall, RAF	Jan 18, 1937
Sqn Ldr R G Forbes, RAF	Apr 27, 1938
Lt Cdr H Gardner, RN	May 24, 1939
Lt Cdr A J Debenham, DSC, RN	Jun 15, 1949
Capt F W Brown, RM	Aug 11, 1941
Unit disbanded	Aug 11, 1942
Lt J A Levers, RN	Oct 1, 1942
Lt Cdr (A) E L Russell, DSC, RNVR	Mar 12, 1943
Lt Cdr G C Edwards, RCNVR	Mar 2, 1944
Unit disbanded	Oct 16, 1944

Stations/Ships
Seletar, HMS *Eagle*, Kai Tak, Penang, China Bay, Kallang, Sembawang, Dekhelia, Maaten Bagush, Fuka, HMS *Illustrious*, Port Sudan, Port Reitz, Machrihanish, North Front, HMS *Argus*, Lee-on-Solent, Abbotsinch, HMS *Activity*, Fearn, Dunino, HMS *Unicorn*, Maydown, Ayr, St Angelo, HMS *Striker*, Grimsetter and Eglinton

825 Squadron

(Nihil obstat (Nothing stops us))
Aircraft

Swordfish I	Jul 1936-Nov 1941
	Jan 1942-Jun 1944
Swordfish II	Mar 1942-Jun 1944
Swordfish III	Jun 1944-Apr 1945

Commanding Officers

Lt Cdr J I Robertson, RN	Jun 8, 1935
Lt Cdr H A Traill, RN	Oct 25, 1935

825 Squadron		
Lt Cdr J I Robertson, RN	Mar 17, 1937	
Lt Cdr A Brock, RN	Sep 11, 1937	
Lt Cdr J W Hale, RN	Aug 19, 1938	
Lt Cdr (A) E Esmonde, DSO, RN	May 31, 1940	
Unit disbanded	Nov 13, 1941	
Lt Cdr (A) E Esmonde, VC, DSO, RN	Jan 1, 1942	
Lt Cdr (A) S Keane, RN	Feb 23, 1942	
Lt Cdr (A) S G Cooper, RN	Dec 15, 1942	
Lt Cdr (A) A H D Gough, RN	Feb 29, 1944	
Lt Cdr (A) F G B Sheffield, DSC, RNVR	May 5, 1944	
Lt Cdr P Snow, RN	Feb 25, 1945	
Unit disbanded	Apr 12, 1945	

Stations/Ships
Amriya, Hal Far, HMS *Glorious*, Gosport, Abingdon, Southampton, Aboukir, Dekhelia, Prestwick, Worthy Down, Detling, Thorney Island, Carew Cheriton, HMS *Furious*, Hatston, Evanton, Donibristle, Lee-on-Solent, Arbroath, HMS *Argus*, HMS *Furious*, Castletown, Abbotsinch, Campbeltown, HMS *Victorious*, HMS *Ark Royal*, Manston, Machrihanish, Andreas, HMS *Avenger*, Fearn, Exeter, Dunino, Stornoway, Stretton, Yeovilton, Hooton Park, Maydown, Ayr, Belfast, HMS *Pretoria Castle*, Kaldadarnes, Inskip, HMS *Vindex*, Limavady, Mullaghmore, HMS *Trouncer* and HMS *Campania*

826 Squadron		
(Iatet anguis in aqua (A snake lies concealed in the water))		
Aircraft		
Swordfish I	Jul 1940-Aug 1940	
	Mar 1941-Sep 1941	
Commanding Officers		
Lt Cdr W H G Saunt, DSC, RN	May 27, 1940	
Lt Cdr J W S Corbett, RN	Jun 24, 1941	

Stations/Ships
Bircham Newton, St Merryn, Campbeltown, Belfast, HMS *Formidable*, Wynberg, Sheikh Othman, Dekhelia, Fuka and Maaten Bagush

828 Squadron		
Aircraft		
Swordfish I	Oct 1941-Nov 1941	
Commanding Officers		
Lt Cdr D E Langmore, DSC, RN	May 6, 1941	

Stations/Ships
HMS *Ark Royal* and Hal Far

829 Squadron

(Non effugient (They shall not escape))
Aircraft

Swordfish I	Jul 1940-Sep 1940
	Mar 1941-Dec 1941
Swordfish II (ASV)	Dec 1941-Oct 1942

Commanding Officers

Lt Cdr O B Stevinson, RN	Jun 15, 1940
Lt Cdr J Dalyell-Stead, RN	Oct 12, 1940
Lt Cdr F M Griffiths, RN	Dec 24, 1941

Stations/Ships
Campbeltown, St Merryn, St Eval, Crail, HMS *Formidable*, Dekhelia, Lydda, Nicosia, Palisadoes, Norfolk, Eastleigh, Lee-on-Solent, Speke, Ternhill, HMS *Illustrious*, Tanga, Port Reitz and Stamford Hill

830 Squadron

(In via gloriae (In the way of glory))
Aircraft

Swordfish I	Jul 1940-Mar 1943

Commanding Officers

Lt Cdr F D Horne, DSO, RN	Jul 1, 1940
Capt K L Ford, RM	Aug 1, 1940
Lt Cdr J G Hunt, RN	Sep 1, 1941
Lt Cdr F H E Hopkins, RN	Dec 6, 1941
Lt Cdr A J T Roe, RN	Jun 7, 1942
Lt A Gregory, RN	Feb 23, 1943
Unit disbanded	Mar 31, 1943

Stations/Ships
Hal Far

833 Squadron

Aircraft

Swordfish I	Dec 1941-Nov 1942
Swordfish II	1942-Jan 1944

Commanding Officers

Lt Cdr R J H Stephens, RN	Dec 8, 1941
Capt W G S Aston, RM	Jan 14, 1943
Unit disbanded	Jan 7, 1944

Stations/Ships
Lee-on-Solent, Gosport, Crail, Hatston, Machrihanish, HMS *Biter*, Stretton, HMS *Avenger*, North Front, HMS *Argus*, Thorney Island, St Eval, Ballykelly, HMS *Stalker*, Dunino and Maydown

834 Squadron	
(Una feriendo delemus (By striking together we destroy)) *Aircraft*	
Swordfish I	Dec 1941-Apr 1943
Swordfish II	Sep 1942-Nov 1944
Commanding Officers	
Lt Cdr L C B Ashburner, RN	Nov 12, 1941
Lt L G Wilson, RN	Nov 20, 1941
Lt Cdr (A) E D Child, RN	Jan 21, 1943
Lt Cdr (A) D W Phillips, DSC, RN	Aug 12, 1944

Stations/Ships
Palisadoes, HMS *Archer*, Floyd Bennett Field, Crail, Exeter, Harrowbeer, Machrihanish, Eglinton, Ballykelly, HMS *Hunter*, North Front, Paestum, HMS *Battler*, Stamford Hill, Katukurunda, Coimbatore, Cochin, Trincomalee and Vavuniya

835 Squadron	
Aircraft	
Swordfish I	Feb 1942-Feb 1943
Swordfish II	Oct 1942-Jun 1944
Swordfish III	Jul 1944-Mar 1945
Commanding Officers	
Lt Cdr M Johnstone DSC, RN	Feb 15, 1942
Lt Cdr J R Lang, RN	Apr 28, 1942
Lt Cdr W N Waller, RN	Sep 15, 1943
Lt Cdr (A) T T Miller, RN	Dec 2, 1943
Lt Cdr E E Barringer, RNVR	Feb 17, 1944
Lt Cdr F V Jones, RNVR	Aug 12, 1944
Lt Cdr (A) J R Godley, RNVR	Jan 15, 1945
Unit disbanded	Mar 31, 1945

Stations/Ships
Palisadoes, Norfolk, HMS *Furious*, Lee-on-Solent, Hatston, Stretton, Machrihanish, HMS *Activity*, Kirkistown, HMS *Battler*, Ballykelly, Eglinton, Ayr, HMS *Argus*, HMS *Ravager*, HMS *Chaser*, Abbotsinch, HMS *Nairana* and Burscough

836 Squadron	
(Mari coeloque (By sea and sky)) *Aircraft*	
Swordfish I	Mar 1942-Feb 1943
Swordfish II	Mar 1943-Jun 1945

836 Squadron

Swordfish III	Dec 1944-May 1945	
Commanding Officers		
Lt Cdr J A Crawford, RN	Mar 1, 1942	
Lt Cdr R W Slater, DSC, RN	Jul 9, 1942	
Lt Cdr J R C Callander, RN	Jun 29, 1944	
Lt Cdr (A) F G B Sheffield, DSC, RNVR	Mar 5, 1945	
Unit disbanded	Jul 29, 1945	

Stations/Ships

Palisadoes, HMS *Biter*, Lee-on-Solent, Machrihanish, Crail, St Merryn, Thorney Island, Ballykelly, Maydown, MV Empire MacColl, Dartmouth, MV Empire MacCabe, Ronaldsway, Belfast, MV Empire MacApline, MV Empire MacMahon, MV Empire MacAndrew, MV Empire MacAndrew, MV Empire MacRae, MV Amastra, MV Empire MacKay, MV Ancylus, MV Empire MacRae, MV Empire MacColl, HMS *Activity*, MV Adula, MV Empire MacAndrew, MV Miralda, MV Alexia, MV Empire MacCallum, MV Empire MacDermott, MV Rapana, MV Empire MacKendrick, HMS *Campania*, Hatston, Belfast, MV Empire MacDermott and HMS *Vindex*

837 Squadron

Aircraft		
Swordfish I	May 1942-Jun 1943	
Swordfish II	Jun 1942-Jun 1943	
Commanding Officers		
Lt Cdr A S Whitworth, DSC, RN	Mar 15, 1942	
Unit disbanded	Jun 15, 1943	

Stations/Ships

Palisadoes, Floyd Bennett Field, HMS *Dasher*, Campbeltown, Lee-on-Solent, St Merryn, Hatston, Crail, HMS *Argus*, North Front, Dunino, Machrihanish, Ballykelly and Eglinton

838 Squadron

Aircraft	
Swordfish I	May 1942-Apr 1943
Swordfish II	Apr 1943-Aug 1943
	Nov 1943-Feb 1945
Swordfish III	May 1944-Feb 1945
Commanding Officers	
Lt Cdr J R C Callandar, RN	May 15, 1942
Lt (A) R G Large, RNVR	Jun 7, 1943
Unit disbanded	Aug 13, 1943
Lt Cdr (A) J M Brown, DSC, RNVR	Nov 1, 1943

838 Squadron

Lt Cdr P Snow, RN	Aug 19, 1944
Unit disbanded	Feb 3, 1945

Stations/Ships
Dartmouth, Alameda Island, HMS *Attacker*, Quonset Point, Machrihanish, Maydown, HMS *Argus*, HMS *Activity*, Belfast, *MV Rapana*, HMS *Nairana*, Dunino, Inskip, Harrowbeer, Worthy Down, Long Kesh, Benbecula, Dallachy, Fraserburgh and Thorney Island

840 Squadron

Aircraft	
Swordfish I	Jun 1942-Mar 1943
Swordfish II	Sep 1942-Aug 1943
Commanding Officers	
Lt (A) L R Tivy, RN	Jun 1, 1942
Lt (A) C M T Hallewell, RN	Apr 21, 1943
Unit disbanded	Aug 13, 1943

Stations/Ships
Palisadoes, Miami, HMS *Battler*, Quonset Point, HMS *Attacker*, Stretton, Machrihanish, Hatston, HMS *Activity*, Maydown and MV *Empire MacAndrew*

841 Squadron

(Lucemus nocte (We shine by night))

Aircraft	
Swordfish I	Jan 1943-Apr 1943
Swordfish II	Jan 1943-Apr 1943
Commanding Officers	
Lt R L Williamson, DSC, RN	Jul 1, 1942
Lt (A) L J Kiggell, DSC, RN	Oct 15, 1942
Lt Cdr (A) W F C Garthwaite, DSC, RNVR	Dec 28, 1942
Lt Cdr (A) S M P Walsh, DSC, RNVR	Jul 2, 1943
Unit disbanded	Dec 1, 1943

Stations/Ships
Lee-on-Solent, Machrihanish, Middle Wallop, Manston, Coltishall, Tangmere and Exeter

842 Squadron (Tantivy)

Aircraft	
Swordfish II	Feb 1943-Jan 1945
Commanding Officers	
Lt Cdr (A) C B Lamb, DSO, DSC, RN	Mar 1, 1943
Lt Cdr (A) L R Tivy, RN	Apr 21, 1943
Lt Cdr (A) G F S Hodson, RNR	Mar 27, 1944

842 Squadron (Tantivy)		
Lt Cdr (A) L A Edwards, RN	Aug 2, 1944	
Unit disbanded	Jan 15, 1945	
Stations/Ships		
Lee-on-Solent, Machrihanish, Hatston, Maydown, Belfast, HMS *Fencer,* Grimsetter, HMS *Furious,* HMS *Indefatigable,* Stornoway, Benbecula, Mullaghmore and Thorney Island		

886 Squadron		
(Vires acquirit eundo (It gains strength as it goes)) *Aircraft*		
Swordfish II	Jun 1943-Oct 1943	
Commanding Officers		
Lt Cdr (A) R H H L Oliphant, RN	Jul 27, 1942	
Stations/Ships		
Eglinton, Machrihanish, HMS *Attacker,* North Front, Paestum and Burscough		

SECOND LINE SWORDFISH SQUADRON

(Aircraft and service dates only)

700 Sqn	
Swordfish I/SP	Jan 1940-Jan 1942
Swordfish	Jul 1943-Dec 1943

701 Sqn	
Swordfish I/SP	Sep 1936-Jan 1940

702 Sqn	
Swordfish I/SP	1939-Jan 1940

703 Sqn	
Swordfish I/SP	Oct 1942-Nov 1942

705 Sqn	
Swordfish I/SP	Jul 1936-Jan 1940
Swordfish III	Mar 1945-Jun 1945

707 Sqn	
Swordfish II	Feb 1945-Sep 1945
Swordfish III	Feb 1945-Sep 1945

710 Sqn	
Swordfish I	-Jun 1945
Swordfish II	Apr 1945-Dec 1945

722 Sqn	
Swordfish	May 1945-Oct 1945

726 Sqn	
Swordfish I	Aug 1943-Dec 1943
Swordfish II	Sep 1944-Nov 1945

727 Sqn	
Swordfish	May 1943-Sep 1944

728 Sqn	
Swordfish I	May 1943-1943
	Jan 1946-Feb 1946
Swordfish II	Feb 1944-Jan 1945

730 Sqn	
Swordfish II	Jan 1945-Aug 1945

731 Sqn	
Swordfish I	Dec 1943-Jun 1944
Swordfish II	Dec 1943-Nov 1945
Swordfish III	Nov 1944-Nov 1945

733 Sqn	
Swordfish I	Jan 1944-Dec 1944
Swordfish II	Sep 1944-Nov 1945

735 Sqn	
Swordfish I	Aug 1943-Mar 1944
Swordfish II	Aug 1943-Jun 1944

737 Sqn	
Swordfish II	Mar 1944-Jul 1945

739 Sqn	
Swordfish I	Dec 1942-Nov 1943

740 Sqn	
Swordfish I	May 1943-Aug 1943

Swordfish II	Sep 1944-Aug 1945
Swordfish III	1945-Aug 1945
741 Sqn	
Swordfish I	Mar 1943-Mar 1945
Swordfish II	Mar 1943-Mar 1945
742 Sqn	
Swordfish	Dec 1943-Oct 1945
744 Sqn	
Swordfish I	Mar 1944-Apr 1945
Swordfish II	Mar 1944-Apr 1945
Swordfish III	Feb 1945-May 1945
747 Sqn	
Swordfish I	Mar 1943-Feb 1944
Swordfish II	Jun 1943-Jul 1943
753 Sqn	
Swordfish I	Dec 1939-Jun 1945
756 Sqn	
Swordfish II	Mar 1944-Feb 1945
759 Sqn	
Swordfish I	Nov 1939-Jun 1941
Swordfish II	May 1943
763 Sqn	
Swordfish I	Dec 1939-Jul 1940
Swordfish II	Mar 1945-Jul 1945
764 Sqn	
Swordfish I/SP	Apr 1940-Sep 1941
765 Sqn	
Swordfish I/SP	May 1939-Jun 1941
766 Sqn	
Swordfish I	Apr 1942-Nov 1944
Swordfish II	Apr 1943-Nov 1944
Swordfish III	Mar 1944-Nov 1944
767 Sqn	
Swordfish I	May 1939-Jul 1940
	Jul 1940-May 1944
Swordfish II	Jan 1943-May 1944
768 Sqn	
Swordfish I	Jan 1941-Dec 1944
Swordfish II	Jul 1943-Oct 1945
Swordfish III	Oct 1944
769 Sqn	
Swordfish I	Nov 1941-Feb 1944
Swordfish II	Oct 1943-Feb 1944
770 Sqn	
Swordfish I	Dec 1939-Apr 1940
771 Sqn	
Swordfish	May 1939-Apr 1945
772 Sqn	
Swordfish I	Sep 1939-Jul 1941
Swordfish II	Oct 1942-Aug 1945
773 Sqn	
Swordfish I/SP	Jun 1940-Apr 1944
774 Sqn	
Swordfish I	Nov 1939-Aug 1944
Swordfish II	Feb 1943-May 1944
775 Sqn	
Swordfish I	May 1941-Jan 1945
Swordfish II	Feb 1944
776 Sqn	
Swordfish II	Jun 1944-Dec 1944
777 Sqn	
Swordfish I	Aug 1941-Feb 1944
Swordfish II	Aug 1942-Feb 1944
778 Sqn	
Swordfish I	Sep 1939-Jan 1944
Swordfish II	Sep 1942-Feb 1945
779 Sqn	
Swordfish I	Oct 1941-Aug 1942
Swordfish II	Oct 1941-Jan 1945
780 Sqn	
Swordfish I	Jun 1940-Jul 1943
Swordfish II	Jul 1943-1944
781 Sqn	
Swordfish I	Sep 1940-Dec 1941
Swordfish II	Mar 1942-Feb 1943
Swordfish TS.3	Mar 1953-Nov 1963
782 Sqn	
Swordfish I	Dec 1940-Mar 1941
Swordfish III	Nov 1946
783 Sqn	
Swordfish I	Jun 1942-Oct 1943
Swordfish II	1942-Jul 1945
785 Sqn	
Swordfish I	Nov 1940-May 1944
Swordfish II	Apr 1942-Feb 1944
786 Sqn	
Swordfish I	May 1941-Dec 1943
Swordfish II	Jun 1942-1943
787Y Sqn	
Swordfish	Jun 1944-Oct 1944

787Z Sqn

Swordfish I	Mar 1943-Jun 1944
Swordfish II	Jan 1943-

788 Sqn

Swordfish I	Feb 1942-Jun 1944
Swordfish II	Feb 1942-Jun 1944

789 Sqn

Swordfish I	Jul 1942-Jun 1943
Swordfish II	Oct 1942-Nov 1945

791 Sqn

Swordfish I	Apr 1942-Dec 1944
Swordfish II	Dec 1943-Jan 1944

794 Sqn

Swordfish I	Aug 1940-Jun 1944
Swordfish II	Apr 1944-Jun 1945

796 Sqn

Swordfish I	Jul 1942-Dec 1943
Swordfish II	Sep 1943-Mar 1944

797 Sqn

Swordfish I	Nov 1943-Aug 1945

RNHF

Swordfish I (W5856)	1993-present
Swordfish II (LS326)	1972-present
Swordfish III (NF389)	1990-present

RAF Swordfish Squadrons
(Aircraft and service dates only)

RAF Front-Line Swordfish Squadrons*

8 Sqn
Aircraft

Swordfish I/SP	Aug 1940-Dec 1940

Stations
Khormaksar

119 Sqn
Aircraft

Swordfish III	Jan 1945-May 22, 1945

Stations
Bircham Newton, St Croix (B.63), Maldeghem (B.65) and Knocke le Zout (B.83)

202 Sqn
Aircraft

Swordfish I/SP	Oct 1940-Jun 1941

Stations
Gibraltar

*Swordfish were also attached to 209, 273 and 613 Squadrons in an operational capacity

RAF Second-Line Swordfish Units
3 AACU; 4 AACU; 9 (Pilots)AFU; AAEE; ASU - No.2 (Cardington), No.3 (Sealand & Shawbury), No.4 (Ternhill); MAEE; MU - No.5, 8, 9, 10, 12, 15, 19, 20, 22, 24, 27, 29, 36, 47 and 82; PD (Sealand); RAE & TTS (later TTU)

RCAF Swordfish Units
(Aircraft and service dates only)
1 NAGS (aka 745 Sqn)

Swordfish II	Mar 1943-Feb 1944
Swordfish IV	Feb 1944-Mar 1945

1 WS & 6 B&GS
743 Sqn

Swordfish II	Mar 1943-Mar 1945
	Sep 1946-Nov 1948

RAAF Swordfish Units
25 Sqn
Aircraft

Swordfish I	Mar 1942-Apr 1942

Station
Pearce

Royal Netherlands Navy
860 Squadron
(*Arcens affligo* (Wading off, I afflict))
Aircraft

Swordfish I	Jun 1943-Nov 1943
Swordfish II	Nov 1943-Jun 1945
Swordfish III	Mar 1945-Jun 1945

Commanding Officers
Lt J van der Toorren, RNethN Jun 15, 1943
Stations/Ships
Donibristle, Hatston, Dunino, Machrihanish and Maydown

Other books you might like:

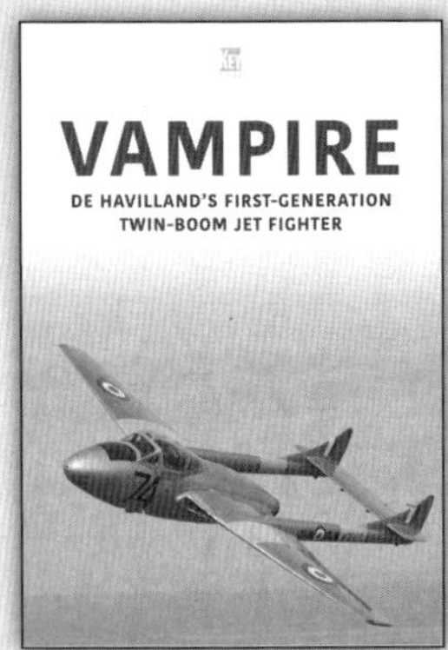

Historic Military Aircraft
Series, Vol. 26

Historic Military Aircraft
Series, Vol. 23

Historic Military Aircraft
Series, Vol. 22

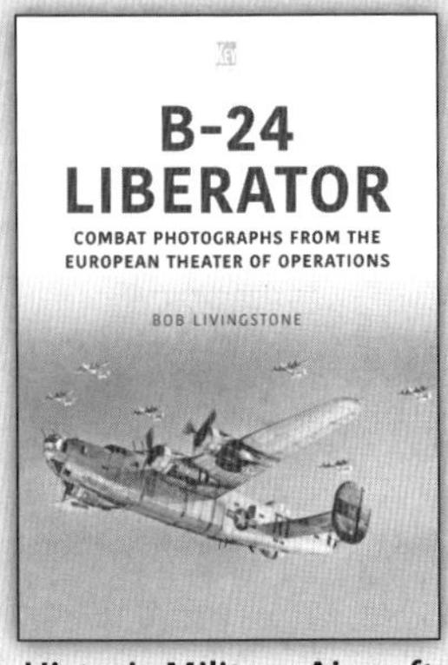

Historic Military Aircraft
Series, Vol. 21

Historic Military Aircraft
Series, Vol. 20

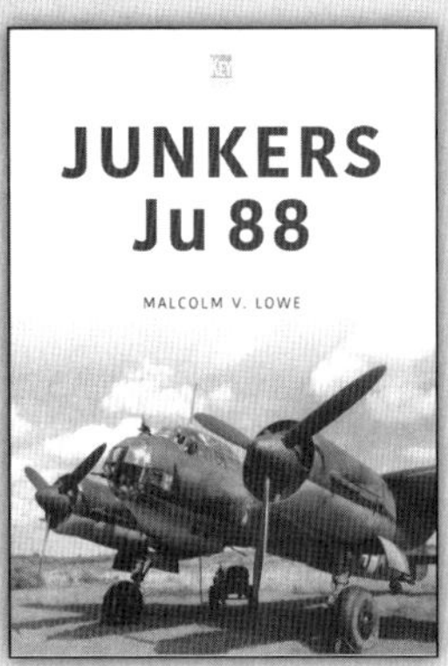

Historic Military Aircraft
Series, Vol. 15

For our full range of titles please visit:

shop.keypublishing.com/books

VIP Book Club

Sign up today and receive
TWO FREE E-BOOKS

Be the first to find out about our forthcoming
book releases and receive exclusive offers.

Register now at **keypublishing.com/vip-book-club**

Our VIP Book Club is a 100% spam-free zone, and we will never share your email with anyone else.
You can read our full privacy policy at: privacy.keypublishing.com